Beyond Ebonics

Beyond Ebonics

Linguistic Pride and Racial Prejudice

JOHN BAUGH

OXFORD
UNIVERSITY PRESS

OXFORD
UNIVERSITY PRESS

Oxford   New York
Auckland   Bangkok   Buenos Aires   Cape Town   Chennai
Dar es Salaam   Delhi   Hong Kong   Istanbul   Karachi   Kokata
Kuala Lumpur   Madrid   Melbourne   Mexico City   Mumbai   Nairobi
São Paulo   Shanghai   Singapore   Taipei   Tokyo   Toronto
and an associated company in Berlin

Copyright © 2000 by John Baugh

First Published in 2000 by Oxford University Press, Inc.
198 Madison Avenue, New York, New York 10016
First issued as an Oxford University Press paperback, 2002.

www.oup.com

Oxford is a registered trademark of Oxford University Press, Inc.

Library of Congress Cataloging-in-Publication Data
Baugh, John, 1949–
Beyond ebonics : linguistic pride and racial prejudice
John Baugh.
p.   cm.
Includes bibliographical references and index.
ISBN 0-19-512046-9; 0-19-515289-1 (pbk.)
1. Black English—United States. 2. English language—United
States—African influences. 3. Slaves—United States—Language—
History. 4. African-Americans—Education—Language arts. 5. Language
and culture—United States. 6. Afro-Americans—Language—History.
I. Title.
PE3102.N42B37   2000
427'.973'08996073—dc21   99-16833

5 7 9 8 6

Printed in the United States of America
on acid-free paper

For Eugene M. Lang . . .
and those whose dreams
he has helped fulfill

Foreword

Why now a book on Ebonics? Hasn't uproar about Ebonics come and gone, a flash in the pan? Yes, but the flash illuminated something in our lives that is still with us, an entanglement of preconceptions about language, race, and fairness that does not go away, that continues to bedevil education and public life. John Baugh patiently traces the early history of the notion, the diverse response when it became a national issue, and how much remains unresolved.

Baugh writes from an especially valuable vantage point. He is trained in sociolinguistics, indeed a prominent figure in the field, known for his own careful study of African American speech and his participation with others in scholarly overviews. He himself is African American, able to draw on his own experience, while speaking matter of factly of being a descendant of slaves. It is especially telling, then, when he faces the continuing power of ignorance and prejudice in our midst.

Most educated people, probably most people, feel they already know what they need to know about language, opportunity, and accomplishment. Most people seem to find it comfortable to think of differences in speech and writing in terms of just two categories, good and bad. They seem untouched by their own experience of diversity according to style and situation, on their own part and that of others. They seem unwilling to consider that some of the differences they encounter may for others be motivated by values and proprieties of social interaction of which they simply are unaware. Empirical study of diversity again and again shows it to involve patterns of appropriateness. For most of us, however, there is just good and bad. And behind "bad," not knowledge of a another pattern, but simply ignorance. Or, still to a considerable extent, inferiority of race.

Since early in the twentieth century, anthropologists and linguists influenced by anthropology have realized that there is no necessary connection between race, language, and way of life. Connections there are of course, but they are historical, not intrinsic. They have realized that all human language is fundamentally equal, in the sense of resulting from a gift universally shared. Particular languages, and varieties of language, of course, are often enough not interchangeable, not equivalent in what they may have been specialized to do or express. But their users share the universal ability to acquire and develop them.

As John Baugh takes us through the mixture of prejudice and good intentions, ignorance and insight, that the Ebonics issue has thrown into relief, he provides something from which we all can learn in attempting to realize in relation to language and education the true promise of this country.

Dell Hymes
Commonwealth Professor of
Anthropology and of English, Emeritus
University of Virginia

Preface

Most people had never heard of Ebonics before December 18, 1996. It was on that date that the Oakland, California, school board passed a resolution declaring Ebonics to be the official language of African American students within that district. Since then much has been written about Ebonics, often equating the term with "black English," "African American vernacular English," or other terms depicting stereotypical language among many American slave descendants.

The linguistic consequences of the African slave trade have been greatly misunderstood, due in part to the social, scholarly, and educational devaluation of linguistic influences and speech that resulted from slavery. That devaluation was further compounded by slave laws intended to stifle black literacy. The Ebonics debate launched another round in a continuing national discussion on how best to educate students for whom standard English is not native.

When Oxford University Press asked me for a book about the Ebonics controversy, I resisted the proposal, fearing that writing such a book would somehow suggest that I advocate Ebonics, which, from a scientific point of view, is problematic. However, I became convinced of the need for this work on January 24, 1997—the day Brent Staples published "The Last Train from Oakland" on *The New York Times* editorial page. I have great respect for Staples, yet I strongly disagree with his distorted linguistic impressions of "broken, inner-city English." His editorial is reproduced here in full:

Editorial Notebook—
The Last Train from Oakland: Will the Middle Class Flee the 'Ebonics' Fad?

The Oakland, Calif., school board deserved the scorn that greeted its December edict declaring broken, inner-city English a distinct, "genetically based" language system that merited a place in the classroom. The policy is intended to build self-esteem for failing students by introducing street language as a teaching tool. In theory, teachers would use street talk as a "bridge" to help children master standard English. But as practiced elsewhere, so-called "ebonics" instruction is based on the premise that street English is as good or better than the standard tongue. This means that students could use urban slang in their schoolwork.

Oakland's attempt to link genes and language was both racist and idiotic. Yesterday's Congressional hearing underscored this point, and brought the city's superintendent under heavy attack. Outraged by the city's proposal, one Congressman suggested restricting Federal aid to the Oakland district.

After the initial barrage of criticism in December, the Oakland board seemed to backtrack, voting last week to drop an explosive passage that spoke of a "genetically based" language. But the board signaled its true intent by saying it would "embrace" broken inner-city English, encouraging children to speak and write it in school. The sanitized resolution is no better than the original. It patronizes inner-city children, holding them to abysmally low standards.

The Los Angeles Times reports that while blacks make up slightly more than half the student population in Oakland, they account for 71 percent of the special-education pupils and only 37 percent of those in programs for the gifted. Educators elsewhere might suggest other remedies—early intervention and tutoring programs, a stronger and more coherent curriculum, a forceful effort to persuade parents to support at home what teachers try to accomplish at school. But the

Oakland resolution recommends nothing of the sort. It is, rather, a 60's-style rant that condemns politicians while absolving parents and communities of any responsibility for failure. It blames the Federal Government for not providing more money. It blames several former governors for rejecting bills that declared so-called "black English" a distinct language. It blames the teachers for not communicating in urban English—and offers them bonuses if they do. Most catastrophically of all, in the name of promoting "self-esteem" the board has conspired to lower the performance bar, declaring all students to be "equal" regardless of whether they have difficulty speaking, reading, writing, or understanding the English language.

The Oakland strategy is in no way unique. As Jacob Heilbrunn illustrates in the Jan. 20 New Republic, so-called "black English"—or "ebonics"—programs have flourished in California schools since the late 1980's, when San Diego began four pilot programs. The programs can be found in San Diego and Los Angeles, where the program is said to reach 31 schools and 25,000 students. "Ebonics" has become a multimillion-dollar affair, with academic theorists, lushly paid consultants and textbook writers all poised to spread the gospel.

Some defenders say "ebonics" functions as a bridge between street and standard English. But in practice, time that should be spent on reading and algebra gets spent giving high fives and chattering away in street language. As a San Diego instructor told *The New Republic*, "If a writing assignment is handed in, written in the home language, the teacher will say 'I like this. This is good. . . . ' They will not say 'This is incorrect.' " "Ebonics" theory licenses this approach. As one of its founders wrote 20 years ago in *The Journal of Black Studies*, the theory avoids giving standard English "a higher status than it deserves."

The Oakland policy will further isolate children who are already cut off from mainstream values and ideas. But its most corrosive effect may be to drive out the middle-class families that keep schools and other institutions afloat. Imagine yourself a parent with the Oakland resolution in one hand, an application to private school in the other— and a streetwise teen-ager to educate. What would you do?

Brent Staples

If he could say such things, what must others think? Immediately I responded with a letter to the editor of the *Times*, published on January

29. I realized then that I had no choice but to begin this book as well.
My letter read:

> To the Editor:
>
> It is regrettable that Brent Staples continues to refer to vernacular African-American English as "broken, inner-city English" and "street English" in his criticisms of the Oakland, Calif., school board for its proposal to treat African-American English as a second language (*Editorial Notebook*, Jan. 24).
>
> Although Oakland's resolutions are poorly worded, it is wrong to misrepresent the unique and profound linguistic consequences of American slavery.
>
> Whereas typical European immigrants may have come to the United States in poverty, speaking a language other than English, they were not enslaved captives who were isolated from other speakers of their native language, which was a practice employed by slave traders to prevent revolts. Nor were they denied statutory access to schools, literacy or judicial relief in the courts.
>
> The Linguistic Society of America has recently affirmed the unique linguistic heritage of American slave descendants, and Mr. Staples's continued misrepresentation of African-American English only serves to perpetuate uninformed linguistic stereotypes.
>
> John Baugh
> Swarthmore, Pa.
> Jan. 24, 1997

Unlike most of my other scholarly endeavors, this venture has been personally painful—both as a linguist, having witnessed the plethora of misinformation that has been widely disseminated about black speech, and as an African American, having witnessed racially divisive rhetoric from both ends of the political spectrum. At the outset, therefore, readers should know that I care much more about the educational welfare of students who lack standard English proficiency than I do about contentious squabbles over moot linguistic terminology.

Beyond Ebonics describes events leading to the crescendo of political, educational, and linguistic events that culminated in a socially discordant fracas when Ebonics first captured broad public attention. The Ebonics skirmish generated considerable consternation and hostility toward any suggestion that African Americans speak a language other than

English. Condemnation of Ebonics was swift and defied ideological compartmentalization: liberals and conservatives alike decried the term. But the birth and evolution of Ebonics, and its journey to public awareness, are informative and worthy of consideration in their own right. This text attempts to clarify several of the issues, misconceptions, and educational policies that emerged from the Ebonics controversy while striving to view them within the broader context of the linguistic legacy of American slavery and to address the linguistic prejudices that tend to inhibit improved race relations.

Readers of this work will, predictably, fall into two broad categories: those who consider Ebonics appalling and those who find it appealing. As with any complex issue where language, race, educational policies, and classroom practices conjoin, the Ebonics controversy defies sound-bite reductionism. That is, each of us reacts differently to linguistic behavior that we hold somewhere between high and low regard.

Because the intended audience for this book spans the entire political spectrum, my personal goals are simultaneously modest and ambitious. I hope this book helps to dispel uninformed and divisive myths about the linguistic consequences of the African slave trade. The prospect that this work might eventually inform rational discussion on how best to educate students for whom standard English is not native is more ambitious but no less consistent with my ultimate aspiration for a future in which linguistic bigotry becomes a relic of the past.

John Baugh
Stanford, California
1999

Acknowledgments

This work is the product of serendipity. By coincidence I participated in a conference sponsored by Oakland's standard English proficiency program, and by coincidence I was a visiting professor at Swarthmore College when news of Ebonics first captured world attention. By coincidence Peter Ohlin, of Oxford University Press, had worked closely with Donna Jo Napoli and Theodore Fernald, who are both faculty members in Swarthmore's distinguished linguistics program. By coincidence, my mentor, William Labov, and Gillian Sankoff were close at hand, as were their students Anita Henderson, Hesham Alim, and Thomas Morton; individually and collectively they initiated a vigorous scholarly conversation about the Ebonics controversy.

In another coincidence this entire episode occurred during semester break, just prior to my teaching a course, "The Evolution of African American English," to a cohort of energetic Swarthmore students who were all extremely capable young scholars. In turn, they unearthed countless obscure references to Ebonics that would have surely escaped my attention without their support and meticulous attention to detail. Eugene M. Lang sponsored my professorship at Swarthmore, and it is to him that I dedicate this work. His devotion to the betterment of those who are less fortunate is evident through his I Have a Dream Foundation. To me, as Swarthmore's Eugene M. Lang Visiting Professor for Issues of Social Change, the timing of these events seemed more than coincidental. Eugene Lang is an exceptional person (having won the United States Medal of Freedom), but his generosity and kindness have also touched my life personally. His dedication to the welfare of humanity has inspired many dimensions of this work.

Swarthmore College President Alfred Bloom and Provost Jennie Keith were former colleagues in linguistics and anthropology when I first met them more than twenty-five years ago, and it was through their leadership and willingness to take risk that I was able and absolutely delighted to return to Swarthmore, where James Michener provided affirmative action funding that allowed me to begin teaching at the college in 1975. Two journalists stand out in my mind in connection with the Ebonics debate—Peter Applebome of *The New York Times,* and James Spady of the *Philadelphia New Observer.* Both men asked extremely insightful questions throughout the Ebonics campaign.

Among my fellow linguists I would like to thank Walt Wolfram; although his significant contribution may be difficult to detect in *Beyond Ebonics,* he offered the earliest detailed suggestions to this work. Similarly, John Rickford, Guy Bailey, James Collins Ida Stockman, John Singler, Carolyn Temple Adger, Anna Celia Zentella, Harry Seymour, Geoff Nunberg, Geoff Pullham, Salikoko Mufwene, Mary Hoover, Orlando Taylor, Marcyleina Morgan, Toya Wyatt, Arnetha Ball, Geneva Smitherman, Ernie Smith, Robert Williams, Elaine Richardson, Tempii Champion, Julie Washington, Lisa Green, Sonja Lanehart, Joshua Fishman, Shirley Heath, Guadalupe Valdés, Kenji Hakuta, Amado Padilla, and many inner-city teachers from the Berkeley, Los Angeles, and Oakland Unified School districts have contributed vastly to my knowledge and understanding of this subject in ways that do not receive sufficient direct recognition within the text.

I am extremely grateful to Dell Hymes, not only for his contribution to this book, but for his close reading of earlier drafts and a host of valuable suggestions. Both he and his wife, Virginia Hymes, have profoundly influenced my life in extraordinary ways that continue to be beneficial to me, my research, and my family.

Nancy Richey deserves special commendation for her careful reading of the entire text. Most professional authors know how valuable outstanding editorial advice can be, and Nancy is one of the finest editors I have known in a writing career spanning more than twenty years. Her vast journalistic and editorial experience consistently cherish the reader, and had she not pointed out early flaws in my logic and representation, portions of this work would have remained too technical or incoherent. I first worked with Nancy during the writing of *Out of the Mouths of Slaves: African American Language and Educational Malpractice* (Baugh 1999), and that professional relationship proved to be so rewarding that I am delighted that Oxford University Press has provided the opportunity for us to work together again.

My deepest thanks go to my family, each of whom sacrificed greatly during the 1996 holiday season when our lives were substantially disrupted by Ebonics tremors that shook our household especially hard. To my children—Ariel, Chenoa, and John—I want to reaffirm my eternal pride, love, and devotion; your help and wisdom far exceed your youth. They too brought Ebonics tales to my attention from obscure schoolyard sources that would have never crossed my radar screen. The ultimate source of support in my life flows from my wife, Charla. She is a person of such extraordinary depth, talent, insight, and compassion that it is nearly impossible for me to fully convey her ultimate contribution to my being. Her willingness to plow through earlier drafts of this work, and others, has always served to sharpen my conceptualization, and her love constantly replenishes my inspiration.

To the staff and editors at Oxford University Press, and especially Peter Ohlin and Jessica Ryan, I wish to express my sincere gratitude for their insight, patience and support.

Contents

Beyond Ebonics

O N E

Linguistic Pride and Racial Prejudice

L abels pertaining to American slave descendants have undergone considerable change over the decades since our forebears were freed. W. E. B. Du Bois observed that racial classifications can be misleading, particularly if those classifications are detested. In 1928 DuBois spoke of these matters in response to Roland Barth, and Barth's advocacy of the change from "Negro" to "colored."

> Do not at the outset of your career make the all too common error of mistaking names for things. Names are only conventional signs for identifying things. Things are the reality that counts. If a thing is despised, either because of ignorance or because it is despicable, you will not alter matters by changing its name. If men despise Negroes, they will not despise them less if Negroes are called "colored" or "Afro-American." (Du Bois 1928:96–97)

Du Bois's sage advice holds true for the Ebonics controversy as well. If the vernacular speech of urban or rural slave descendants is devalued, modified nomenclature will not increase its worth in the eyes of those who hold black speech—or African Americans—in low regard. Many

1

who criticized Ebonics did not do so merely because they objected to the term; they scoffed at Ebonics as an attempt to legitimize "bad English" in the name of politically correct linguistic enlightenment. Detractors often claimed to be offended, resentful, or worse.

On the other hand, Ebonics advocates were elated by efforts to elevate its stature, because they had never equated black speech with "improper English," and they embraced "Ebonics" as a term that could offer linguistic legitimacy and enhance cultural pride among American slave descendants.

Were this tale one of mere labels it might be brief, but Ebonics was first used nearly a quarter of a century ago by African American scholars who objected to "black English." The scholars met at a 1973 conference, "Cognitive and Language Development of the Black Child," hosted by Robert Williams (who coined the term "Ebonics"). In an editorial titled "Ebonics as a Bridge to Standard English," Williams stated, "We met to define our language" (Williams 1997a). Here is the way the conversation went on January 26, 1973:

ROBERT WILLIAMS: We need to define what we speak. We need to give a clear definition of our language.

ERNIE SMITH: If you notice, every language in the world represents a nation or a nationality. What we are speaking has continuity not only in the United States, but outside the United States and all the way back to the mother country. We need to get the term completely off the English scale and start calling it what it really represents.

ROBERT WILLIAMS: Let me make a point here. Language is a process of communication. But we need to deal with the root of our language. What about Ebo? Ebo linguistics? Ebolingual? Ebo Phonics? Ebonics? Let's define our language as Ebonics.

THE GROUP: That sounds good.

ROBERT WILLIAMS: I am talking about an ebony language. We know that ebony means black and that phonics refers to speech sounds or the science of sounds. Thus, we are really talking about the science of black speech sounds or language. (Williams 1997a, p. 14)

The original Ebonics definition is described more fully in the next chapter, but from a linguistic point of view, Ebonics—as originally constituted—refers to a complex mixture of European and African languages born of the African slave trade. How, then, did this original definition become transformed? How did it come to focus more narrowly on the speech of U.S. slave descendants—and are slave descendants in Brazil, the Dominican Republic, or Haiti to be included or excluded from Ebonics? Stated in other terms, does Ebonics refer to one language or to more than one language?

Within the United States a portion of this answer is ideological, because the federal government has never formally acknowledged that slave descendants represent a "language minority population" (see Baugh 1998). Therein lies part of the motivation to declare that "Ebonics is not a dialect of English," and that "limited English proficient (LEP) African American pupils are equally entitled to be provided bilingual education and English as a second language programs to address their LEP needs" (Smith 1998:58).

Although considerable time has elapsed since Oakland educators passed their controversial Ebonics resolution, many of the linguistic and educational problems they articulated have yet to be resolved. These educational impediments are still with us, as American students from all walks of life have been shown to be less well prepared than the vast majority of students from other advanced industrialized countries.

It would be myopic and wrongheaded to pursue educational reforms for African American students in a social vacuum, and I will attempt to consider broader educational implications as we contemplate ways to increase linguistic tolerance among all Americans. But in this instance, those larger educational goals derive from the Ebonics debate that focuses exclusively on the linguistic behavior of African Americans.

Readers of this book presumably seek an informed yet dispassionate survey of Ebonics, but it would be misleading to suggest that I approach this topic with complete linguistic objectivity. Although I bring more than twenty years of linguistic analyses to this subject, I spent my early childhood in inner-city communities where standard English is rare, and those experiences have shaped my life and professional work in ways that defy disengaged objectivity. Thus, this topic is one that remains deeply personal.

To a certain extent, my experiences were similar to those of fellow black students who attended overcrowded, underfunded, inner-city schools. However, unlike many of my childhood peers, I had the advantage of being raised by well-educated parents who were activists on my behalf at school and who strongly encouraged the academic importance of standard English.

Despite the obvious benefits of living in a home with well-educated parents who vigilantly stressed the importance of "proper English," I was also surrounded by friends and neighbors who did not exhibit or prize these linguistic virtues. One of the episodes my parents often recount—an incident I simply don't recall—demonstrated just how firmly I had embraced their steadfast advocacy of standard English.

When I was three or four, one of the older Sisters from our church paid a social call on my parents. Seeing me, she exclaimed, "You sho' is a fine young man." To which I was said to reply, "Are! You *are* a fine young man." My parents retell the story emphasizing both their pride and embarrassment—after all, I was using standard English, which they valued, but my comment could also be interpreted as a sign of precocious impertinence and disrespect for my elders. Fortunately for all of us their friend was undaunted and unfazed; she simply said, "You sho' is."

Beside such episodes, that otherwise escape my memory, lie the earliest linguistic recollections that were sculpted by numerous social encounters with others in the black neighborhoods of Philadelphia where we lived. Back then, during the 1950s, I knew nothing of the distinction between blue-collar and white-collar jobs, but my parents were younger than many of our neighbors, and we were one of a few families that owned a car. The apparent economic abyss between those who rely exclusively on public transportation and those who own their own cars was one of the first sociological distinctions I recall, and I came to this realization long before attending school.

There were early signs of racial and linguistic differentiation as well. For example, I routinely observed that my mother would speak differently to various people on the telephone. She would typically answer any incoming call with a neutral "Hello," and then her speech would shift; if she responded formally—typically to a white person—her speech would become more standard, and if she spoke to a black person, her speech would sound more natural and relaxed. Even her body language would change during the phone calls; her posture during the formal calls was far more rigid and tense than was the case when she would speak to friends or relatives, and her facial expressions would

likewise reflect these differences. Again, these were some of my earliest
memories of linguistic observations, and I lacked the experience, knowledge, or understanding to fully comprehend the significance of her linguistic modifications.

Beyond the sanctuary of our home, the social and linguistic performances I observed were wildly diverse, spanning the loud antics of
hip teens who lived in the neighborhood in contrast to the prim speech
of older gracious Sisters at church, which ritually reinforced mainstream
social, linguistic, and family virtues. Language was often mentioned in
these hallowed gatherings; elders chided those with foul mouths and
vile language who held forth beyond the sanctuary of the good God-
loving folk who attended church. In my youthful mind I extended this
linguistic parable; those who spoke "good English" were supposed to be
emulated; those who spoke "bad English" were not.

At a young age, then, I received mixed messages about language;
some were overt, advocating that I "speak properly" and avoid "bad language," whereas others were more subtle, reflected by the hippest Sisters
and Brothers who emphatically rejected "white speech." I was perplexed.
On what basis should I develop my personal sense of linguistic pride,
and how would it relate to the looming "racial prejudice" that older peers
told me existed in "white" neighborhoods? Because my parents worked
in professional contexts, they had much more contact with whites than
did most of our other neighbors, who had few social contacts beyond
our African American community. My parents were mindful of racial
prejudice, but they were equally concerned that I not be consumed by
racial paranoia, especially so early in life. Long before racial equality
became a highly visible national concern, they sought to instill in me
the color-blind ethos that is our national creed; they taught me and my
siblings that all people are created equal, and that it was our collective
good fortune to live in a country with *the potential* of providing liberty
and justice for all. Their love and wisdom initially shielded us from the
burdens of racial bigotry, and as we grew older they gradually began to
prepare us to withstand the barbs of antagonistic racial hostilities.

Their color-blind mythology was never truly challenged in my youth
because few white students were enrolled at the inner-city elementary
schools I attended. Thus most of my classmates and I weren't constantly
reminded of racial divisions or potential white versus nonwhite conflicts,
although the vast majority of our teachers were white. Like my parents

and the elders at church, these teachers strongly endorsed standard English, and, thanks to the diligent efforts of my mother, I was able to improve my reading even though many of my teachers did little to encourage or fully develop my full academic potential.

Were it not for my parents' love and educational intervention I could have easily been counted among the millions of African American students who never achieved standard English proficiency. But I faced an added sociolinguistic paradox; I didn't want to sound "lame" (see Labov 1972), and, as I had observed "on the corner," most of the "cool brothers" could "talk the talk"—and those who exhibited urban eloquence never did so in standard English. What, then, was I to do? Should I use standard English, to the exclusion of African-American vernacular speech norms, and risk ridicule or social rejection from my black peers? Or, should I resist my parent's standard English advocacy and suffer the domestic consequences of open linguistic rebellion at home? I gradually began to compromise, employing nonstandard speech among my friends while using standard English (to the best of my ability) in church and at home. I confess that my linguistic behavior at school fluctuated greatly. Bad grades were not tolerated in the Baugh household, yet—not wanting to appear either lame or too eager to "act white" (see Fordham and Ogbu 1986)—I became a linguistic chameleon, seeking to avoid speech that would call attention to itself, depending on my immediate circumstances. I felt as though I were trapped in a cultural vise consisting of two opposing linguistic barricades with each side offering situationally dependent rewards or sanctions.

It is also important to acknowledge that my linguistic circumstances changed drastically in 1958. My father had accepted a job in Los Angeles, and we moved from a black neighborhood to one that was in racial transition. Upon arriving in Los Angeles I encountered a strange new world with neighbors who were learning English as a second language. I vividly recall my own racist reactions of linguistic superiority as I listened to them struggle to use English—a "superiority" I tried to exploit in attempts to gain favor among my new African American neighbors and classmates.

Having grown up as a "baby boomer" in black neighborhoods in Philadelphia, my African American male friends and I would play military "war games" against classical American foes. In essence, we considered any enemy of John Wayne's to be our enemy. After all, we had all been weaned on westerns and World War II movies that tended to reinforce some unfortunate racist stereotypes and hypotheses that I projected on many of my new "foreign" California neighbors.

My immediate reaction of racist skepticism was met in turn by cautious curiosity from the almond-eyed children who stopped playing with their hula hoops just long enough to stare at me, "the new kid." Without fully understanding my emotions at the time, I experienced my own burgeoning racism, which was continually reinforced each time I heard a "funny accent."

A few weeks after we arrived in Los Angeles it was time for school, and not only was I the new kid in my class, but I was "fresh meat" for the local bullies, who promptly shattered any false hopes I had about making new friends. However, because of my misplaced youthful sense of cultural and linguistic superiority, combined with my lack of experience or tolerance of people who were unfamiliar (i.e., people who were not black), I only considered the prospect of making new black friends.

I was not only insensitive to many of my fellow classmates who were learning English as a new language, I was also occasionally cruel. I found their speech awkward, and their funny accents served as a source of considerable linguistic amusement. In an effort to endear myself to my fellow African Americans I began to mimic the speech of nonblack students who were struggling to learn English; these racist antics were rather pitiful displays that I hoped would impress my fellow black classmates, most of whom remained quite unimpressed. Rather than change tactics, I opted to turn up the volume, which led to some personal confrontations—many centered around language and my misguided sense of linguistic superiority.

My presumptuous sense of linguistic grandeur resulted mainly from the considerable value Mom and Dad placed on the importance of standard English and speaking properly, and at home I did my best to conform to their linguistic preferences. But away from home my youthful quest to become "cool" at the expense of other minority students was unfortunate, and just as shameful as any distasteful form of racial bigotry. In retrospect I can now admit to myself, and others, that I was somewhat "lame"; but because I aspired to be "hip," I concluded that the road from nerdiness to greater popularity (particularly with my black peers) could be paved with linguistic and racial insults against other minority students whose English proficiency was inferior to mine. Each day young verbal warriors would gather in the schoolyard, exchanging taunts, jeers, and various insults before an audience of onlookers who would take considerable delight at the spectacle of this, generally, bloodless sport. Girls were often among the best combatants or instigators— and some girls were clearly superior, with the eloquence and timing to devastate any and all comers who were foolish enough to engage them in verbal or physical battle.

Lacking the skill to face off against the best among the schoolyard verbal gladiators, I sought less challenging linguistic prey on which to hone my—less than adequate—oral dueling skills. One incident in particular provided a personal epiphany that shaped my future as a linguist.

The verbal insults that were daily ritual displays at our school conformed to certain routines. Teachers and school administrators hoped we would play organized games before school and at recess or before school, and they typically provided jump ropes, basketballs, tetherballs, and kick balls for this purpose. Inevitably, during the course of a game or some other hostile encounter, two or more students would begin hurling insults, which typically began with the phrase, "Yo' Mama. . . ." This utterance rarely resulted in an immediate fight, although there were noteworthy exceptions. The more common response would be, "Don't be talkin' 'bout my Mama, 'cause yo' Mama done. . . ." At that point a group of spectators would inevitably surround the joust, and upon any such gathering then ever greater numbers of students would drop whatever they were doing to watch any escalating confrontation. Students often had the luxury of choosing among several conflicts.

On the day in question I happened to be drawn into the center of the ring. My adversary, Carlos, was considerably larger than I, but English was quite new to him, which magnified my skewed sense of linguistic superiority. We were having an honest disagreement about the game we were playing until he withheld the ball, which stopped play altogether.

> JB: C'mon, man, give me the ball.
> C: I'll give the ball to yo' Mama, punk.
> JB: My Mama ain't got nothin' to do with this, man, just give me the
>   damn ball!

The confrontation escalated, becoming louder and more vulgar, and Carlos turned up the insults in his best rendition of a vulgar urban vernacular, claiming that my mother had excessively large breasts. I, of course, took considerable umbrage and responded in kind, with equally distasteful comments about his mother and her sexual proclivities. In the process I not only insulted his mother but mimicked his Latino accent, which infuriated him even more.

At that time I was relatively small—and quite small in comparison to Carlos. To my physical detriment, Carlos decided it was time to stop talking and start fighting, and he began to give me the "ass whippin' '" he and his fellow Latinos and Latinas felt I deserved—and they may have been right. I knew that my linguistic mockery was cruel, but I was too young to fully comprehend their anger, nor did I really care at the time. I wish I could say that I held my own during the fight, but that would be a lie. Carlos was a far more skilled fighter than I, and— although I kept spewing verbal insults—I beat a fairly hasty retreat to the relative safety of our classroom, where the teacher, a middle-aged white man, overheard me "badmouthing" Carlos.

Teacher: John: Stop it.

JB: Hey man! He's hitting me. I ain't doing nothing.

Teacher: You're making fun of him.

JB: Yeah, but he's hitting me, I'm just talking.

Teacher: But you're making fun of the way he talks, so stop it.

JB: (*shucking and jiving in my best rendition of exaggerated standard English*) I'm very sorry, I didn't realize I was doing anything wrong.

Teacher: Now, John, why don't you speak that way all of the time and improve yourself?

The teacher failed to realize what my black peers sensed immediately; namely, my rendition of standard English was an overt attempt to mock the teacher and standard English with one blow. He assumed I was being contrite—not sarcastic, and his statement regarding my linguistic self-improvement was intended to reinforce the virtues of speaking standard English, which had little linguistic usefulness or value among the African American peer group I so desperately wanted to impress.

It was at that moment that my personal linguistic epiphany occurred: When I was insulting Carlos—by mimicking his dialect—the teacher interpreted it as an authentic linguistic affront, but when I attempted to sarcastically insult the teacher—through my exaggerated rendition of standard English—he concluded that I was being apologetic, deferential, or perhaps both.

Much like the fabled one-eyed man in the land of the blind, I felt an absolute sense of linguistic superiority over my classmates for whom English was not native. Not only were they learning English as a new language, they were also doing so in ways that placed them at considerable linguistic disadvantage in the ritualized verbal bouts that consumed so much of our youthful recreational activity.

The talent I possessed, to mimic the nonstandard dialects of my peers, was not initially developed for the educational and scholarly causes I have come to endorse as a professional linguist, but that mimicry provided early exposure to the combinations of racial prejudice and linguistic pride—or shame—that lie at the heart of the Ebonics controversy.

I share these observations, in part, because readers should be fully aware of my early childish sense of linguistic superiority over my classmates and neighbors who were learning English as a new language, along with my racist reactions to their speech. In a real sense my uninformed negative response to learners of English as a second language was similar in nature to many of those who chastise African American vernacular speech norms. Having previously straddled the fence between linguistic dexterity and racial bigotry, I saw both sides of these issues long before Williams and his associates created the term "Ebonics." Smitherman (1978) speaks eloquently of her own linguistic trauma at the hands of speech pathologists who equated her black speech with cognitive disabilities, and Smith (1975) describes the linguistic contexts in which he took great pride in his capacity to employ vernacular African American speech at the same time that he repudiated "white speech." Even conservative African American pundits who lament affirmative action speak at length about their personal sense of linguistic shame (see chapter 9, in this volume).

It is against this backdrop of linguistic devaluation that Ebonics was born, and the next chapter provides an in-depth survey of the genesis of Ebonics and the social and linguistic circumstances that brought it to life. But during those early years, when Ebonics was first introduced, it was nurtured in racially segregated contexts that offered limited exposure beyond the community of African American scholars who embraced the term and celebrated its Afrocentric conceptualization (Tolliver-Weddington 1979).

That racially sheltered incubation was shattered when Oakland educators, at the behest of the Oakland African American Educational Task Force, chose to adopt Ebonics as the official language of their students of African descent (see chapter 3), but the content of the resolutions adopting Ebonics evoked a firestorm of controversy. The wording of their original resolution proved to be so controversial that they eventually retracted much of its content, producing a substantially revised resolution that attempted to deflect the anger and angst that Ebonics critics directed at the Oakland school board (see chapter 4).

Although many legislators and parents continue to express strong support for more "school choice" along with simultaneous advocacy of greater local authority over school decisions, many balked when Oakland's local school officials demonstrated such choice by choosing Ebonics. Government officials at every level, from local school boards and municipalities to various state legislators, as well as members of Congress and the secretary of education, rejected Ebonics. Politicians of every political persuasion detected the pervasive sense of public outrage against Ebonics, and a flurry of legislative activities to banish Ebonics were spawned shortly after the media had lost interest in the topic (see chapter 5).

But much of the legislative effort to drive a spike through the heart of Ebonics was so broad, or so poorly worded, that many of these anti-Ebonics bills fizzled (see chapter 6). In retrospect it is clear that the vast majority of politicians were eager to drop this controversial and racially evocative topic in favor of other pressing business. Once Oakland educators had abandoned Ebonics there was little justification to pursue the matter. One African American legislator noted that passing laws to abolish educational programs based on Ebonics would be akin to passing laws to banish liquor sales in churches; they would be superfluous.

Still other reasons that Ebonics legislation failed, were related to competing definitions of the term (see chapter 7). Due largely to its ideological origin (see chapter 2), Ebonics has come to mean different things to different people. Professional linguists did not begin to use the term until after Oakland's resolution (O'Neil 1998), and even when some did, typically they were unaware of its origin—or the fact that Williams (1975) and his colleagues had defined Ebonics quite differently from the most common interpretation in the United States.

The combination of the media spotlight, race, language, education, and politically correct dogma soon leapt beyond the political realm and became fodder for comedians, pundits, and editorial cartoonists (see chapter 8), and "-bonics" soon became a productive suffix as off-color Ebonics jokes began to flourish. Daytime and late-night talk shows began to lampoon Ebonics and those who continued to champion its educational utility. Some of those reactions were racist, providing bigots with a license to engage in the type of overtly racist rhetoric that was far more common during the bygone era of blatant racial segregation. But many African Americans mocked Ebonics too, including Maya Angelou, Bill Cosby, and Kweisi Mfume, among others. It would therefore be simplistic and wrong to paint Ebonics supporters or detractors in contrastive racial terms.

Of considerable relevance to this debate are some qualitative results from a national linguistic survey completed shortly after the Oakland school board passed its infamous Ebonics resolution. That survey attempted to determine what groups favored or disfavored Ebonics and why. The results of the survey—which include observations that African Americans who endorse Ebonics tend to reject racial integration—have prompted me to devote the conclusion of this book to promoting linguistic tolerance in our national quest for racial reconciliation. Blacks who dislike Ebonics tend to value racial integration. Slave descendants who favor Ebonics were also in favor of racially segregated schools, as long as those schools are fully funded and free to adopt an Afrocentric curriculum. African American Ebonics detractors, for the most part, disfavor the prospect of racially segregated schools.

Ironically, the national dialogue on race has sidestepped the Ebonics controversy, but few other topics that have captured global attention on a comparable scale have more to do with the linguistic and educational themes that are central to America's struggle toward racial reconciliation. Ebonics, by virtue of its African American classification and Oakland's efforts to adopt it for educational purposes, lies at the vortex of public education and national race relations. Until such time as leaders in positions of political authority have the collective courage, vision, and wisdom to redress the linguistic legacy of American slavery within the context of providing equal educational opportunities to all children, we will never be able to fully overcome our long history of race-based inequality.

Ebonic Genesis

'Tis but thy name that is my enemy.

Shakespeare, *Romeo and Juliet*

In January 1973 Robert Williams hosted a conference in St. Louis titled "Cognitive and Language Development of the Black Child." Two years later he published *Ebonics: The True Language of Black Folks.* There he defined Ebonics in the Pan-African tradition of W. E. B. Du Bois. Over two decades later, Williams affirmed the international foundations of his linguistic creation. During testimony before the U.S. Senate (see chapter 5), he stated:

Ebonics has two major dimensions as a language:
1. A lexicon or the vocabulary of the language,
2. Morphology or the study of the structure and form of the language that include its grammatical rules. Ebonics may be defined as the linguistic and paralinguistic features which on a concentric continuum represent the communicative competence of the West African, Caribbean, and United States slave descendent of African origin. It includes the grammar, various idioms, patois, argots, ideolects, and social dialects of Black people.(Williams 1975:vi)

As this original definition indicates, Ebonics is the linguistic and para-linguistic consequence of the African slave trade. It developed in West Africa, as well as throughout the former European colonies of North and South America wherever slaves were sold into bondage. Ebonics, under this earliest definition, was never intended to apply narrowly to the United States—and therein lies part of the confusion that has resulted from the Ebonics controversy.

Before coining "Ebonics," Williams was best known for his research on standardized IQ tests, and his long-standing critique of racial bias—particularly against blacks—embodied in traditional standardized norm-referenced IQ tests. He devised a series of alternative tests, including the Black Intelligence Test of Cultural Homogeneity (BITCH), which proved to be controversial for some because it intentionally inverted racial bias in favor of African Americans. Nevertheless, black children did score significantly higher on the Ebonics version than on the standard English version. The following two examples show Williams's method of code switching or translation:

1. Standard English: Mark the toy that is behind the sofa.
EBONICS: Mark the toy that is in back of the couch.
2. Standard English: Point to the squirrel that is beginning to climb the tree.
EBONICS: Point to the squirrel that is fixing to climb the tree.

As Williams explains:

What I discovered was that, in the first example, the words [*sic*] "behind" and "sofa" were blocking agents. I translated both words to "in back of" and "couch." In the second example, I translated the term "beginning" to "fixing to." These changes produced dramatic positive changes in the children's test scores. (Williams 1997b:3)

Herein lies another significant source of linguistic controversy: The "Ebonics translations" are not exclusive to African Americans. Are the terms "in back of" or "couch" or "fixing to" unique to Ebonics? No, they are not; rather, they represent colloquial or regional dialect variations that unquestionably exceed black America. Most native speakers of American English—regardless of race—might use the expression "in back of the couch." Others, especially in the South, could easily use the expression "fixing to" with the identical meaning that Williams attributes to Ebonics.

As one who has long been critical of racial bias in standardized tests, I am sympathetic to Williams's aspirations for racially neutral ones, especially in such "high stakes" tests as the Scholastic Assessment Test (SAT) or the Graduate Record Examination (GRE). However, greater linguistic specificity is essential to eliminating test bias. Such "translations" may have closed gaps in standardized test scores between black and white children, but they expose important linguistic problems pertaining to the definition of Ebonics, especially if one claims that Ebonics is unique to African Americans (Smith 1992, 1998). Considerable care and more precise attention to linguistic details must therefore be forthcoming from those who endorse and advocate Ebonics. The transformation of Ebonics from its international origins to its global unveiling as pertaining to Oakland's students of African descent has resulted in competing international and domestic Ebonics definitions. This process took more than two decades, and a host of political, legal, educational, and linguistic ingredients simmered within a racial pressure cooker that eventually exploded (see chapters 5 and 7, in this volume).

Momentarily we shall see that social science, education, legislation, and the law come together in the Ebonics debate, but none of these fields can abide multiple definitions for the same concept, and Ebonics has come to acquire a Janus face. The task of documenting the historical and contemporary linguistic consequences of American slavery is a fascinating enterprise, made all the more difficult by the combination of an oral history, racism, and a legacy of educational and social apartheid that still lingers despite the abolition of slavery. Excessive attention to "Ebonics," per se, could distract us from developing a more complete and accurate sociohistorical portrait of the linguistic legacy of American slavery.

Given the linguistic and geographical domain encompassed by the African slave trade the first two criteria associated with Williams's original Ebonics definition are characteristic of all languages. By his early definition, the "lexicon" or "vocabulary" of Ebonics varies considerably from one region to another, particularly as those regions include all the areas from which slaves were captured, as well as the areas to which they were eventually transported and sold. And because the slave traders came from different European countries, their language backgrounds added to this linguistic complexity; that is, beyond the linguistic attributes contributed by slaves through their various native African languages.

The second tenet, dealing with "morphology," is more complicated because the "structure and form" of many languages exceed the "grammatical rules" that are relevant to their morphology. Morphology describes the smallest meaningful units of a language, including prefixes and inflections. Morphemes, which are either "bound" or "free," combine in specific ways to form the lexicon of a language, which must then conform to syntactic rules that govern grammaticality.

The popular myth that Ebonics or black English is ungrammatical (rather than nonstandard) complicates this picture even further, which is why the Linguistic Society of America adopted a misunderstood resolution affirming the logical and grammatical coherence of vernacular African American English (see appendix A). Semantic considerations are also linked to morphology and the lexicon because different semantic interpretations can lead to considerable confusion during an ordinary conversation, particularly if the interlocutors speak with different dialects.

Like others who have miscast the educational attributes of vernacular black English (see Orr 1987), Williams is not a linguist—as revealed by his explanation for the significantly divergent performances elicited from either formal and colloquial renditions of nearly identical standardized test items. Again, it is erroneous to declare or imply that Williams's translations are the exclusive linguistic province of American slave descendants; there is no empirical justification for such a claim. Nevertheless, despite the specificity of Williams's original Ebonics definition in relationship to the international linguistic legacy of the African slave trade, the examples commonly used to illustrate Ebonics tend to not include nonstandard African dialects derived from contact with other European languages spoken by slave traders (e.g., French, Dutch, or Portuguese).

Beyond the linguistic realm I am quite sympathetic to Williams's desire to include "paralinguistic features" within his primordial Ebonics definition. However, such paralinguistic behavior continues to defy precise measurement and therefore exceeds the scientific boundaries to which linguists typically adhere. Although many linguists would concede that it is important to consider paralinguistic behavior in any comprehensive evaluation of human communication, linguistic science is not yet suitably equipped to measure and interpret such a phenomenon with the same precision it can bring to bear on other spoken or written forms of human language.

How, then, have we arrived at the current state of terminological affairs—where Ebonics has come to be characterized so differently from its original international definition? Part of the answer to this question lies in the realm of linguistic predisposition. Over time, due largely to political considerations, the definition of Ebonics drifted from its preliminary international classification to a narrower U.S. domestic interpretation. Blackshire-Belay (1996) pushed the Ebonics pendulum back toward Africa and beyond its slave origins to include the entire African diaspora, further complicating efforts to pin down Ebonics or how best to define alleged linguistic homogeneity among those of us who share African ancestry.

Returning briefly to the birth of Ebonics, it is both interesting and ironic that few of the African-American authors who contributed to Williams's book ever employ the term. In fact, the term appears sparingly in only three of the twelve chapters of *Ebonics: The True Language of Black Folks*. The label "Black English" is far more common throughout the book in which Ebonics was first introduced. Even terms such as "black language" and "black discourse style" occur more frequently.

Why is this the case? Why would authors use "black English" rather than "Ebonics," especially in a book that embodies the linguistic debut of Ebonics? Williams offers additional reflective insight into the nature of the scholarly deliberations that resulted in his call for Ebonic terminology. During the 1973 conference, which consisted exclusively of African American scholars,

> a barrage of criticism held that the concept of Black English or nonstandard English contains deficit model characteristics, and therefore must be abolished. Following considerable discussion regarding the language of Black people, the group reached a consensus to adopt the term Ebonics (combining Ebony and phonics or Black sounds). (Williams and Rivers 1975:100; see chapter 1)

Williams and Rivers (1975:107) were primarily concerned with cognitive issues, and they were especially critical—as am I—of research based on IQ tests indicating that some racial groups are mentally superior or inferior to others. Most social scientists have long been aware of cultural bias in standardized tests, and Williams and Rivers stated that their "present findings clearly militate against the less language or deficiency hypothesis put forth by Bernstein (1961), Bereiter and Engleman (1966), and Jensen (1969)." Due in part to the primacy of Williams and Rivers's cognitive concerns, their linguistic hypotheses were not only secondary but overstated.

Although there is ample justification for a comprehensive international definition that encompasses the linguistic consequences of the African slave trade, Ebonics has received so many definitional face-lifts that it is almost impossible to recognize from a linguistic point of view. Neither journalists nor U.S. Secretary of Education Richard Riley was aware of these definitional iterations; otherwise they would not have been so quick to equate Ebonics with black English or vernacular African American English. The Oakland resolution of December 18, 1996, which catapulted Ebonics onto the world stage, was explicit in this regard, stating that "Ebonics is not a black dialect or any dialect of English."

Part of the ensuing confusion, and anger, triggered by the Ebonics controversy grew directly from the term's multiple definitions. Some of these inconsistencies exist in the Afrocentric literature that purports to support Ebonics; others resulted from detractors of Ebonics, who have equated it with "slang," "broken inner-city English," "bad English," or worse. Indeed, the seeds of these terminological inconsistencies can be found in Williams's original text, as well as in some of the ensuing writings by professional linguists who, in their haste to embrace Ebonics, failed to fully articulate the international foundations of the term.

How one defines Ebonics is more than mere semantic quibbling: Educators who have embraced Ebonics to refer to the language of American slave descendants certainly do not intend to suggest that black students in urban and rural schools throughout the United States speak the same language as did their slave descendants in Haiti or Brazil. The language of African descendants in each of these nations has its origins in the African slave trade, to which Williams originally referred.

The early Ebonics literature, written by proponents of Ebonics prior to the national confusion regarding competing terminology, is inconsistent about its intended referential domain. Broad definitional convolution helped to accentuate the linguistic consternation that inadvertently propelled the Ebonics controversy. For instance, whereas Smith once equated Ebonics with black English, he eventually recanted that position when he stated the following:

> [T]o the extent that they have historically been born into, reared in, and compelled to live in socially separate linguistic environments, i.e., from Euro-American English speaking people, African-Americans have, in fact, retained a West and Niger-Congo African thought process which is manifested in the substratum phonology, morphosyntax, and semantic-lexemic structure of their speech. Therefore, the native language of African-American people is not English. It is Ebonics, the linguistic continuation of Africa in Black America. (1975:77)

He further asserts:

> Ebonics is not "genetically" related to English, therefore, the term Ebonics is not a mere synonym for the more commonly used term "Black English." If anything the term is, in fact, an antonym for Black English. (Smith 1992:41)

In many respects "Ebonics" has suffered the same linguistically misperceived fate as the term "sign language." Linguists are quick to note that American sign language and British sign language are separate and distinctive languages. Whereas American English and British English constitute different but more or less mutually intelligible English dialects, American sign language and British sign language are not mutually intelligible, especially not in ways that are comparable to their spoken English counterparts. Despite this reality, many nonlinguists tend to use the general term "sign language" without further specification.

The same has been true for Ebonics. Since the vast majority of people from all walks of life first encountered Ebonics in news reports, they equate it with "black English." In much the same manner that linguists distinguish among different sign languages, it would have been far more accurate for scholars, Oakland educators, and journalists to refer to (North?) "American Ebonics" rather than "Ebonics"—which, like the term "sign language," has overt international implications.

Some Ebonics advocates have reaffirmed the international foundations of the term: Ebonics in the United States, Ebonics in Haiti, Ebonics in Brazil, and Ebonics in Africa should not be equated with a single language. There is no empirical linguistic justification for such consolidation. However, Ebonics, as a linguistic construct derived from the linguistic consequences of the African slave trade, is of considerable scholarly utility—despite inconsistencies in previous accounts, and regardless of its saturation with political and ideological baggage that can no longer be easily disposed of.

On this last point, consider, for example, Smith's highly controversial statement:

> The failure or ineffectiveness of many classroom teachers, even those who have attempted to show some genuine concern and sensitivity to the plight of African American children by having sought and obtained what they believed was culturally specific and relevant information, has been due to their use of inappropriate teaching methods and strategies which were predicated on misinformation from the implied or explicit white supremacist postulates of such authors. . . . (1992:39)

Other discussions that advocate Ebonics have gone so far as to castigate linguists of African descent who did not previously embrace the term:

> Even African scholars writing about language have been captured by the same aura of European dominance and have written out of the same paradigm. Thus popular and well-known scholars of language and linguistics have often written from the standpoint of the received paradigm . . . even some of the best theorists have been trapped by the categories of European domination. (Blackshire-Belay 1996:5,6)

In my opinion such assertions are inaccurate and overstate the case. For example, black scholars introduced the term "African American English" (Smitherman 1991), and they did so considerably before Jesse Jackson's public proclamations on the topic (see Baugh 1991).

Linguists of African descent, and those who have studied the linguistic consequences of slavery, diverge considerably regarding opinions about Ebonics and how best to evaluate the available corpus of limited historical evidence. Many of the leading black linguists did not attack Oakland but instead attempted to increase public awareness of black English, the black English trial, and the educational plight of poor African-American students who have not yet mastered standard English (see Perry and Delpit 1998).

Blackshire-Belay (1996:7) preceded the Oakland controversy, casting Ebonics into a different mold. She observed the following:

> [T]he theoretical foundation for this approach has been laid out in the Afrocentric scholarship emerging from the Temple School, which in turn is described as "the Afrocentric School of Thought," or the understanding of the black experience as an extension of African history and culture. The Afrocentric paradigm engages ideological questions with both insight and intellectual audacity. (1996:20)

Blackshire-Belay (1996) conveys the promise and peril of such an overtly ideological approach. The promise lies in her careful reaffirmation of the international "family tree of Ebonic languages," which is consistent with the international definition Williams first formulated in 1973. The peril, however, lies in her unequivocal adherence to racial heritage as integral to her revised Ebonics definition:

> To best understand this very complex process, this author [Blackshire-Belay] finds it helpful and advantageous to provide an illustrative example of the following nature: In a practical sense we can say that to "ebonize" a language is to view the Ebony tree in the Ancient World (Africa) bearing fruit in the form of letters, syllables, and words of phonetic, morphological, and syntactic value. Nonverbal communication patterns in African culture, for example, rhetorical style, body movement, expressions, gestures, are included in the process as well. . . . I extend the term Ebonics to include *all* languages of African people on the continent and in the Diaspora that have created new languages based on their environmental circumstances. (Blackshire-Belay 1996:20)

Within this expanded definition one would include all indigenous African languages under the Ebonics banner, as well as any language spoken by people of African descent. The resulting conceptualization overtly links African heritage to (multilingual?) Ebonics. This broadened definition elevates racial unity, but it does so at the expense of linguistic accuracy. It also places a tremendous burden on educators and scholars who might otherwise seek to employ the term. Even though there may be considerable justification for using a single label to refer to the linguistic consequences of the African slave trade—as no such term existed before Williams coined "Ebonics"—it is another matter altogether to suggest that every indigenous African language and all ensuing languages spoken by people of African descent should supersede the definition Williams originally adopted.

The vast majority of linguists of African descent have carefully and precisely characterized and classified the linguistic behavior of black people in various regions of the English-speaking world, and Blackshire-Belay—to her credit—offers a valuable account of African languages and their typology. But in so doing, she (and others) has created elastic definitions of Ebonics that ultimately undermine scientific validity. Educators, including those in Oakland who welcomed Ebonics with open arms, were ill served by the existence of multiple definitions. For some, the affirmation of Afrocentric Ebonics interpretations proved to be especially enticing, and several well-intentioned educators eventually embraced Ebonics with considerable zeal—only to discover that many Americans were hostile to their efforts and pedagogical intentions.

THREE

A Contentious Global Debut

On December 18, 1996, the Oakland, California, school board propelled Ebonics into the global spotlight by passing a resolution defining Ebonics as the native language of 28,000 African American students within that school district (see chapter 4). Since then supporters and detractors alike have waged massive campaigns championing their respective positions. Advocates continue to claim that formal recognition of Ebonics will enhance educational prospects for black students and bolster their literacy and mastery of standard English (Smith 1998). Detractors, on the other hand, dismiss any effort to legitimize Ebonics or its alleged educational benefits.

Personal linguistic histories and other cultural experiences shape the range of opinions on this topic. Whatever your stand on Ebonics, others with equally strong convictions are likely to hold opinions that differ considerably from yours. Figure 1 illustrates this sociolinguistic relativity. Supporters and detractors are defined as those who, respectively, endorse or abhor Ebonics, and these diverse opinions are then projected across a range of racial backgrounds.

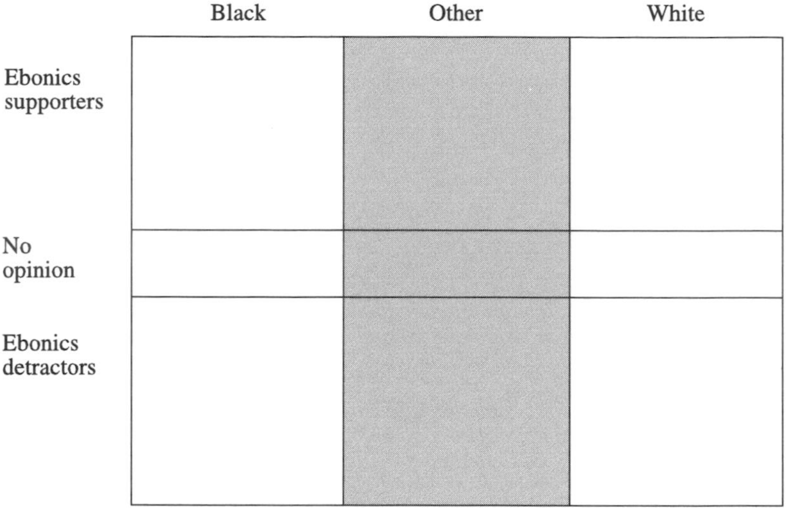

Figure 1. American sociolinguistic relativity among supporters and detractors of Ebonics.

Readers are encouraged to identify their own position within figure 1; shaded areas encompass those (e.g., Native Americans and Hispanics) who do not fit easily into the black or white categories.

Nine categories emerge from figure 1, six of which are most relevant to Ebonics: black, white, and other supporters of Ebonics and black, white, and other detractors of Ebonics. Within each of these groups, differences of opinion arise regarding the potential benefits of racial integration or segregation, which are not inherently central to Ebonics preferences or dislikes. Before turning to descriptions of these six groups, however, readers are encouraged to reflect on an additional factor: timing. When did you first hear of the term "Ebonics"; was it before the Oakland school board passed its resolution on December 18, 1996, or after that date?

Many of the black supporters of Ebonics were aware of the term long before the Oakland school board introduced it into the global lexicon, and therein lies significant interpretive diversity. Proponents of

Ebonics—and some blacks most explicitly—view it as a source of linguistic pride for African Americans. Those African Americans who endorse Ebonics, whenever they first heard the term, share the belief that it embodies the linguistic heritage of black Americans and, as such, could have considerable educational merit.

Whites who support Ebonics are few. Moreover, such whites tend to express their endorsement of Ebonics within a larger context of educational dissatisfaction; that is, they remain critical of an educational status quo that has provided so many African American students with an inferior education. A common refrain among white supporters is simply that we should "give advocates of Ebonics a chance to prove their point." This "wait and see" attitude grows from a sense of frustration, if not exasperation, regarding the long-standing educational practices that have failed to help the majority of black students meet with greater academic and professional success.

Supporters who are neither black nor white find striking similarities between the educational needs of African American students and that of language-minority students (i.e., students for whom English is not native). The original and revised Oakland school board resolutions extol this view, largely by drawing analogies between (and essentially equating) the educational and linguistic circumstances of black students with those of many Native American, Hispanic American, and Asian American students (see chapter 4).

The vast majority of Ebonics detractors were unaware of the concept until after the infamous Oakland resolution, and the vast majority of people who are now acquainted with the term tend to reject it, fluctuating between mild and forceful disdain. Some of the most ardent critics of Ebonics are African American. Many already know of the derogatory public commentaries by Maya Angelou, Bill Cosby, and Kweisi Mfume shortly after the Oakland school board passed the controversial resolution.

Blacks who recoiled at the concept did so for a variety of reasons. Some found the wording of the resolution objectionable; others rejected the idea that "Ebonics is not a black dialect or any dialect of English" (The original Oakland Ebonics Resolution, Dec. 18, 1996). Others felt that the teaching of Ebonics to students—from any background—constituted a retrograde step in American education. We shall return to some of these concerns momentarily, but one of the most apparent outcomes of the Ebonics controversy is that it exposed wide differences of linguistic opinion among American slave descendants.

Whites who reject Ebonics span the entire political spectrum from liberals to conservatives. Whereas white liberals who decry Ebonics have often done so with a sense of remorse, many white conservatives have viewed the entire episode as an "end run" attempt to circumvent efforts to dismantle affirmative action. White racists and other extremists have exploited Ebonics through vulgar web sites and jokes that lambaste non-standard English in various ways (see chapter 8).

Those critics of Ebonics who are neither white nor black include many of the Native Americans, Hispanic Americans, and Asian Americans the Oakland school board had hoped to enlist as allies. Far from viewing African American Ebonics as linguistically and educationally analogous to their linguistic heritage, many of these critics felt that the Oakland school board was trying to abscond with the limited bilingual education funding available to students for whom English is not native. This was clearly the concern of Secretary of Education Richard Riley, who released a statement condemning the Oakland resolution at the same time he rejected any anticipated request for bilingual education funding for African American students. Because bilingual education funds are reserved for students who do not speak English, Secretary Riley's assertion that black students are indeed native speakers of English amounts to a clear declaration that they are ineligible for Title VII federal funding allocations (Baugh 1998).

Critics and supporters of Ebonics can also be found beyond the national borders of the United States. Scholars in Europe, Asia, Canada, and elsewhere who are familiar with the unique linguistic heritage of African Americans have on occasion defended the Oakland school board. However, many residents from other countries consider the Ebonics debate as evidence of blacks in America seeking "special treatment" at the expense of nonblacks. These global reactions are particularly relevant because American citizens have immigrated to the United States from every corner of the globe; this history of linguistic diversity helps to account for alternative interpretations of this topic.

How, then, have Americans from both similar and dissimilar social, ethnic, and racial backgrounds come to view Ebonics so differently? Part of the answer to this question lies in the various ways and degrees to which U.S. citizens have "melted into the pot." And because linguistic behavior is an essential channel for acculturation, it figures prominently in understanding how Ebonics managed to touch such a raw nerve in the body politic.

Americans from every background should never forget a vital linguistic fact. Hundreds of indigenous languages thrived in what is now the United States long before Europeans ever set foot on these lands. The disintegration of Native American languages was inversely related to the rise of English as the dominant national language. English fluency is now essential to successful participation in contemporary American society. These are matters of historical linguistic record that are not in dispute. Thus, readers may appreciate that the current treatment of linguistic integration applies to colonial and postcolonial linguistic development of nonindigenous immigrants only.

Linguists tend to identify "standard" dialects or languages as political constructs, having little to do with their inherent linguistic structure. A universal principle of sociolinguistics maintains that speakers who hold positions of political influence and economic power are the very individuals who set linguistic standards. In older civilizations, these standards were determined by royalty; vestiges of those highly stratified societies exist in Europe, Asia, Africa, and elsewhere. By extension, in former colonies—such as Australia, Brazil, South Africa, and the United States—the current national standards have been cast in the shadows of former colonial languages that once politically dominated the social landscapes.

Such has been the case for postcolonial North and South America and, in particular, for the United States as a nation that was once composed of former British, French, Dutch, and Spanish colonies. Because the current thesis focuses more narrowly on the Ebonics controversy and the unique linguistic history of American slave descendants, we shall concentrate here on cases that magnify the existence of racialized linguistic consternation in the melting pot.

Figures 2 and 3 portray the broader pattern of linguistic integration within the United States, including current residents and their ancestors. These illustrations try to convey some of the regional and social diversity that was brought by colonists, immigrants, and others who settled within the continental United States. The Pilgrims and other English-speaking immigrants who came from England are not illustrated, but it is important to recognize that those early English-speaking

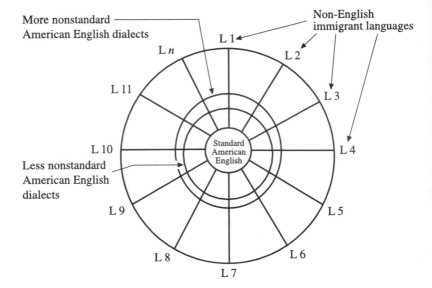

Figure 2. A generic model of linguistic acculturation among former immigrants to the United States.

settlers established the regional American dialects we associate with older upper-class families throughout the original thirteen colonies. Some of these older families, due to the wealth they accumulated along with corresponding political influence, came to be the very speakers who established local linguistic standards. Although their speech was drawn from the outcast dialects of England, it was able to acquire elite provincial stature within the colonial context.

Thus the establishment of American standard English differs considerably from the establishment of British standard English, which traces its beginnings to the speech of royalty. Such was the case throughout Europe: Royalty influenced linguistic standards in Spain, France, Germany, Russia, and elsewhere. In essence, these royal linguistic norms represent the standards by which these languages are evaluated today in Europe; however, they differ considerably from the neolinguistic standards by which these languages are judged today in such former European colonies as Algeria, Australia, Brazil, Canada, India, Mexico, and the United States.

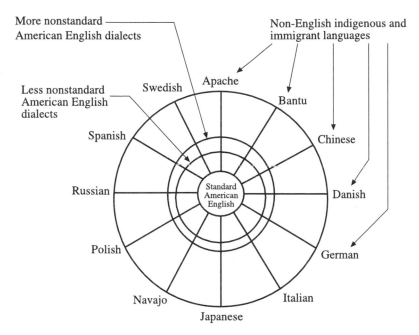

More nonstandard American English dialects

Non-English indigenous and immigrant languages

Less nonstandard American English dialects

Apache

Swedish

Bantu

Spanish

Chinese

Russian

Standard American English

Danish

Polish

German

Navajo

Italian

Japanese

Figure 3. An authentic model of acquisition of American English by non-English speakers.

Early settlers to Massachusetts, Pennsylvania, and Virginia, in particular, came from different dialectal regions in England and eventually gave birth to the upper-class dialects of American English that survive among those states' oldest families of distinction. Indentured servants, who followed thereafter from Scotland, Ireland, and Wales, often spoke uneducated nonstandard English dialects. The most critical distinction among different immigrant speakers of English lies not in their particular countries of origin but, rather, because in the fact that enslaved Africans—unlike English settlers and many indentured servants—came to America against their own free will and with no prior knowledge of English.

Here, the history of American education assumes significant relevance because slaves, along with the indigenous Indian population, were denied access to schools by law. In essence, then, restrictive laws that prohibited access to education actively kept enslaved Africans illiterate. During the colonial period, the notion of compulsory education was still a dream and often advocated on the grounds that the aimless roaming children of "foreigners" were a major social concern. Schools were then thought to be a place to train children to become citizens who shared similar values and customs. Blacks and many others, including women, were denied equal access to schools and tended to be excluded from the "best" schools. Early in this nation's history Puritan schools were for the Puritans, Quaker schools were for the Quakers—and the fate of those who somehow were denied the benefits of a good education was at the mercy of the forces of social Darwinism, whose effects confirmed the dictum that "the rich get richer." Nevertheless, this grand land of opportunity became a magnet for immigrants simply because one might eventually ascend beyond the rigid social class barriers they had left behind in "the old country."

In the sharpest of contrasts to these voluntary immigrants, slaves had no legal rights under the law, and our contributions to the birth of the nation have always been slighted in comparison with the educated elite. Many, but not all, of these elite citizens—men who composed the landed gentry—were hypocrites in simultaneously denying many of my African ancestors the very freedom and liberty they demanded as revolutionaries from their English monarch. Thomas Jefferson is perhaps the most symbolic harbinger of this historical paradox. This irony rarely escapes American slave descendants or others who share Dr. King's dream of racial equality.

Most Americans reflecting on their own personal ancestry can likely identify those ancestors who spoke languages other than English, or who spoke nonstandard English, when they first came to America. Not only would they have been victims of linguistic discrimination within the larger society, they would also likely have been branded with derogatory labels. Whether arriving without papers ("w.o.p.," as they were entered in the immigration records) or with little money, such immigrants suffered indignities of derogatory group labels in addition to social and linguistic discrimination based on their "strange" accents. So it was under such discrimination that other early immigrants—such as Dutch, Germans, Spanish, and French—along with the slaves, confronted the challenges of learning English as a secondary language.

Still, only African Americans have suffered the indignities of slavery. No other mothers who have immigrated to this land have ever been forced to accept the statutory prospect that their children could be sold as property, with no legal recrimination or recourse against owners who could sell, abuse, or kill those children under the full protection of slave law. Perhaps some slave owners were kind to their slaves, but there were no laws preventing them or their peers from being exceedingly cruel to their slaves. Indeed, the mere existence of slavery as an institution is sufficiently cruel that one need not articulate the physical brutalities that were sanctioned by law against slaves and their posterity (see Higgenbotham 1978, 1998). Blacks were the only immigrants who were also denied statutory access to schools and literacy, and the linguistic consequences of slavery contain the seeds from which the Ebonics controversy was born.

Figure 2 presents a generic model of postcolonial linguistic integration for immigrants who spoke languages other than English. This model is somewhat misleading because Americans were not fully aware of a national spoken standard for American English until after the comparatively recent invention of radio. Yes, a written form of standard American English, as apart from "the King's English," began to emerge with print technology, but standard spoken English, as enunciated by Edward R. Murrow and his peers, and as heard on radio in ordinary homes throughout the nation, practically revolutionized the spoken American standard. For the first time Americans from coast to coast could hear the same voices and often at the same time.

The typical immigrant to the United States arrived in poverty, often speaking a language other than English, represented by the outer ring of Figure 2. They spoke a language—or languages—represented by numbers 1 through n. The outer ring also represents the first generation of immigrants to the United States whatever the year of that immigration. That first generation of immigrants began a linguistic journey toward standard American English, mediated by such infrastructural technologies as radio, represented by the "bull's-eye" of this linguistic target. Depending on many variables yet to be elaborated, these first immigrants usually learned some form of nonstandard English that was strongly influenced by their native language. Many of these first- and second-generation immigrants to the United States were openly mocked because of their accents or "broken English," a term familiar to most readers but linguistically bankrupt, because linguistic science does not recognize any language or dialect as inherently superior or inferior to any other.

This model fails to take another psychological variable into account, namely, the extent to which immigrants were either proud or ashamed of their linguistic and cultural heritage. The model also does not capture the extent to which such pride, or shame, may have been conveyed in the privacy of the home but concealed from others during public gatherings. It also does not reflect the reverse sociolinguistic phenomenon of one immigrant group disparaging another, which I observed as a child growing up in Los Angeles among my Chinese American and Japanese American neighbors. Many first-generation immigrants were made to feel ashamed of their speech and cultural heritage, but later generations often take considerable pride in their ancestral language, despite the fact that English may be their first and only language. My Asian American neighbors created private schools and extracurricular programs to ensure that their children would retain their native language. And, as the cultural tensions in some of Amy Tan's novels reflect, many Asian Americans were not eager to marry other Americans who did not share their racial ancestry. So this trend, which differed from that of typical European immigrants, reflected a combination of racial discrimination against Asian Americans and their own cultural predisposition toward racial purity.

Be that as it may, white immigrants who changed their names often did so to conceal their heritage. They felt that discrimination and prejudice were so prevalent that they were willing to conceal their heritage by abandoning their family names, and in so doing they could escape detection. Many immigrant families discouraged their children from speaking the language of "the old country." The justification for this discouragement was clear: "Real" Americans speak fluent English. Thus German, Polish, Russian, French, and Italian, among others, were not considered to have any linguistic capital in the United States, where English was clearly the dominant language of education and professional discourse. Many of the concerns that are now raised about languages other than English, brought by new immigrants, previously confronted German, Italian, and other immigrants who arrived at the turn of the twentieth century. They too were the victims of subtle, and not so subtle, linguistic discrimination as Newell's (1908) childhood tale, *The Hole Book,* amply illustrates. Every nonstandard immigrant dialect is negatively portrayed, as is African American English. Newell's message to every child was absolutely clear; those who spoke English with a strange accent did so at their personal peril. Many immigrants were free to exercise their First Amendment rights by speaking languages other than English, but to do so to the exclusion of learning (standard?) English would constrain socialization to the linguistic ghettos of the ethnic neighborhoods in which the languages from the old countries continued to thrive.

Eventually, descendants of this first generation would come to learn English as their mother tongue. Figure 2 illustrates a continuum between nonstandard English and the standard English that ensuing generations of immigrants learned as their primary language. They would often do so with distinctive dialects that were influenced by their social class and the region of the country in which they lived, as well as traces of the accents that were spoken by their parents and grandparents who, again, are represented by the outer ring of languages. However, the case of blacks who eventually could pass for white notwithstanding, slave descendants could not merely change their names or their speech patterns to conceal their heritage in the hope of escaping discrimination and improving their personal prospects.

Figure 3 is more specific, identifying several of the languages spoken in North America before colonization, as well as many of the languages that were brought here by voluntary, as well as involuntary, immigrants (see Ogbu 1978, 1992). As with Figure 2, this model implies that standard American English is the central target of language and dialect acquisition. However, American linguistic standards can be cast in both national and regional terms. The national standard, as previously stated, may be reinforced through broadcast speech, whereas regional standards can be traced to the old upper-class families who still speak with strong regional dialects. Many of our senators and congressional representatives reflect these regional standards in their speech.

Figure 3 hints at two important issues that the generic model of Figure 2 does not capture: First, the specific immigrant language shapes the nonstandard dialect that follows it along the trajectory toward standard English; second, differential attitudes toward groups that occupy some of the other spokes on Figure 3's wheel help to explain the history of linguistic consternation in the melting pot. Many Americans are keenly aware that they are the direct beneficiaries of their forebears' sacrifice and hard work in the face of discrimination, and they do not understand why black Americans should hold a different outlook. Although the overt discrimination that once allowed slavery and de jure racial segregation no longer prevails, conceptual gaps about racial discrimination are some of the major factors responsible for growing efforts to defend or dismantle affirmative action.

More blacks than ever have achieved positions of social prominence, thereby suggesting that racial barriers no longer justify the educational underachievement of African Americans or, by extension, of other citizens of color who were once the victims of overt discrimination. Viewed in this light, it is easy to comprehend the linguistic consternation that Ebonics has evoked in the minds of its many detractors, for they see it as both moving in exactly the wrong educational direction and being racially divisive. After all, black Americans do not have a monopoly on nonstandard English, as illustrated in Figures 2 and 3. So, why should we assume that black students who speak nonstandard English are any different from other immigrants who speak nonstandard English (see Sowell 1997; chapter 9, this volume)?

In actuality, this is the very essence of the Ebonics controversy: are African Americans linguistically similar or dissimilar to other immigrants who came to the United States speaking languages other than English? Oakland's preliminary Ebonics resolution draws direct linguistic comparisons between black students and immigrant students for whom English is not native, claiming that both should have equal educational rights under the law. However, as we now know, the linguistic history of American slave descendants is unique and not truly comparable to any other voluntary group of immigrants (see Ogbu 1978, 1992).

F O U R

Oakland's Ebonics Resolutions

Substantial linguistic evidence indicates that slave descendants of African origin should not be equated with other U.S. immigrants, but the law has never addressed the consequences of our unique linguistic heritage. One reason many politicians responded forcefully, and negatively, to Oakland's Ebonics assertions arose from concerns that the school district was poised to ask that those consequences be redressed through bilingual education funding for African American students.

Smith (1998) affirmed this view by stating that "LEP (i.e., limited English proficient) African-American pupils are equally entitled to be provided bilingual education and ESL (i.e., English as a second language) programs to address their LEP needs" (p. 58). While linguists continue to argue over distinctions between "a language" and "a dialect," these classifications have direct statutory and funding implications for educators and legislators who must implement corresponding policies.

Although the media was caught by surprise by Oakland's Ebonics resolutions, educators and scholars already familiar with California's Standard English Proficiency (SEP) program for speakers of black language were fully aware that many educators who were devoted to the educational advancement of African American students had enthusiastically embraced Ebonics and integrated it into their teaching—teaching that adopted ESL strategies to build pedagogical scaffolds between the vernacular that is prevalent among many African Americans and standard English or mainstream U.S. English (see Lippi-Green 1997).

Mary Hoover (1998), the former dean of education at Howard University who also served as an educational adviser to Oakland's SEP program, observed that "many who condemn Ebonics refer to it as 'bad grammar,' 'lazy pronunciation,' or slang" (71). She goes on to clarify Oakland's SEP program, asserting that it "stresses Ebonics as a bridge to teaching literacy to African-American students. Its emphasis is on teaching students Standard English speaking skills, on teaching the teachers about the Ebonics speakers' language and culture, and on teaching reading through 'Superliteracy,' which endorses phonics in addition to eight other components" (p. 73).

Whereas many school districts simply turned a blind eye to the linguistic legacy of American slavery, members of the Oakland school board, and Toni Cook in particular, took some decisive steps that ultimately gave rise to the Ebonics debate (see Perry and Delpit 1998). The Oakland Unified School District is one of the only urban school districts in the nation where the majority of students are African American, and Cook was dissatisfied with the educational plight confronting all students within the district. Unaccepting of the educational status quo, she initially sounded local alarms by calling for the formation of a task force to address the educational problems that she and other Oakland educators found objectionable:

> Six months ago, I asked the superintendent to form a task force that would look at the performance and achievement issues of African-American kids. In the six years I've been on the board, every index of performance and achievement has gone down for African-American kids. And those [sic] statistics that you wanted to go down were going up. (Leland and Joseph 1977:78)

The African American task force, in turn, produced the following policy statement, which adopts the first formal statement of the controversial interpretation that Ebonics is a language other than English:

Policy Statement

There is persuasive empirical evidence that, predicated on analysis of the phonology, morphology, and syntax that currently exists as systematic, rule governed and predictable patterns exist in the grammar of African-American speech. The validated and persuasive linguistic evidence is that African-Americans *(1) have retained a West and Niger-Congo African linguistic structure in the substratum of their speech and (2) by this criteria are not native speakers of a black dialect or any other dialect of English.* (emphasis added)

Moreover, there is persuasive empirical evidence that, owing to their history as United States slave descendants of West and Niger-Congo African origin, to the extent that African-Americans have been born into, reared in, and continue to live in linguistic environments that are different from the Euro-American English speaking population, African-American people, and their children, are from home environments in which a language other than English language is dominant within the meaning of "environment where a language other than English is dominant" as defined in Public Law 1-13-382 (20 U.S. C. 7402, *et seq.*).

The policy of the Oakland Unified School District (OUSD) is that all pupils are equal and are to be treated equally. Hence, all pupils who have difficulty speaking, reading, writing or understanding the English language and whose difficulties may deny to them the opportunity to learn successfully in classrooms where the language of instruction is English or to participate fully in our society are to be treated equally regardless of their race or national origin.

As in the case of Asian-American, Latino-American, Native American and all other pupils in the District who come from backgrounds or environments where a language other than English is dominant, African-American pupils shall not, because of their race, be subtly dehumanized, stigmatized, discriminated against or denied.

Asian-American, Latino-American, native American and all other language different children are provided general funds for bilingual education, English as a Second Language (ESL) and State and Federal (Title VII) Bilingual Education programs to address their needs arising from limited English proficiency or no English proficiency (LEP or NEP).

African-American pupils are equally entitled to be tested and where appropriate, shall be provided general funds and State and Federal (Title VII) bilingual education and ESL programs to specifically address their LEP/NEP needs.

All classroom teachers and aides who are bilingual in Nigerian Ebonics (African-American Language) and English shall be given the same salary differentials and merit increases that are provided to the teachers of the non-African-American LEP pupils in the OUSD.

With a view toward assuring that parents of African-American pupils are given the knowledge base necessary to make informed decisions, it shall be the policy of the Oakland Unified School District that all parents of LEP (limited English Proficient) pupils are to be provided the opportunity to partake of any and all language and culture specific teacher education and training classes designed to address their child's LEP needs.

On all home language surveys given to parents of pupils requesting home language identification or designations, a description of the Districts' programmatic consequences of their choices will be contained.

Nothing in this Policy shall preclude or prevent African-American parents who view their child's limited English proficiency as being non-standard English, as opposed to being West and Niger-Congo African language based, from exercising their right to choose and to have their child's speech disorders and English Language deficits addressed by special education and/or other District programs.

Taking the last paragraph first, parents are given the option of classifying their African American children into one of two linguistic categories: students who speak "non-standard English," and students who are "West and Niger-Congo African language based," for the purpose of selecting among various programs within the district. Moreover, the policy statement is quite explicit that (Nigitrian) Ebonics is not "a black dialect or any other dialect of English." Direct comparisons to "Asian-American, Latino-American, Native American, and all other language different children" as being "provided general funds for bilingual education, English as a Second Language (ESL) and State and Federal (Title VII) Bilingual Education programs" appear to contradict denials by some

Oakland school officials of their intentions to pursue federal funding to expand the SEP program.

Although John Ogbu, a renowned professor of anthropology, served as a member of Oakland's African American task force, no linguistic experts served on that committee. The strongest linguistic influence came in the form of consultations with Ernie Smith (1992, 1998), who staunchly advocated Ebonics as something other than English. It was he who offered linguistic advice to members of the Oakland African American task force regarding the wording of the preceding policy statement and subsequent Ebonics resolutions, which drew directly and heavily on his emphatic disassociation between Ebonics and black English; as previously observed (see chapter 3), Smith asserts the following:

> Ebonics is not "genetically" related to English, therefore, the term Ebonics is not a mere synonym for the more commonly used term "Black English." If anything the term is, in fact, an antonym for Black English. (1992:41)

It is on this fundamental point that most linguists strongly disagree (see O'Neil 1998); if Ebonics is to have any linguistic credibility it should not be defined in opposition to "black English" or "African American vernacular English," or other like terms that refer neutrally to the linguistic behavior of most American slave descendants. Any suggestion that American slave descendants speak a language other than English is overstated, linguistically uninformed, and—frankly—wrong.

Because I know many dedicated Oakland teachers personally, including many who have been devoted to the principles of teaching standard English as espoused within Oakland and California's SEP program, I was unwilling to condemn their efforts when I was contacted by journalists. I was confident, based on previous personal meetings and conversations with several Oakland educators and residents, that they would not knowingly do anything to harm the educational welfare of students in their charge. It was based on this first-hand knowledge that I expressed technical linguistic reservations, but without chastising educators whom I know nurture and respect their students:

> Professor Baugh said that he had reservations about viewing Ebonics as a separate language, but that there should be resources to deal with

black linguistic distinctiveness. "It would be misleading for the public to equate the language of the descendants of slaves with the linguistic problems of new immigrants from Russia," he said. "But having said that, there are very few instances where school districts have adequately tried to address the linguistic consequences of slavery. The people involved here have the best interests of the students at heart, and I think it's unfair to be exceedingly critical on linguistic grounds when they're trying to help." (*New York Times*, Dec. 19, 1996, p. A19.)

Most linguists, myself included, are unaccustomed to volatile public controversies, but the media circus that followed Oakland's December 18, 1996, Ebonics resolution witnessed the rare sight of linguists leaping from their well-worn armchairs to clarify the systematic and rule-governed nature of African American vernacular English, or Ebonics. By remarkable coincidence, the annual meeting of the Linguistic Society of America (LSA) followed on the heels of the Oakland resolutions and Secretary Riley's preemptive rejection of anticipated requests for bilingual funding.

Those linguists who gathered in Chicago early in January 1997 at the LSA convention were, by coincidence of timing, compelled to consider the Ebonics controversy. After considerable deliberation, the members voted unanimously in favor of a resolution primarily intended to affirm the linguistic integrity and legitimacy of American slave descendants (see appendix A).

I was somewhat surprised to learn that the LSA had not only incorporated the term "Ebonics" into its resolution but, perhaps inadvertently, did so as if Ebonics and black English were synonymous: "The variety known as 'Ebonics,' 'African American Vernacular English,' and 'Vernacular Black English' and by other names is systematic and rule-governed like all natural speech varieties." Because of the tremendous professional diversity among various linguistic specialists, few of the linguists gathered at the annual meeting were aware of Afrocentric Ebonic definitions or their explicit rejection of prevailing linguistic terminology (see Blackshire-Belay 1996; Smith 1992). It is important to note here that the LSA resolution of January 1997 and the Oakland resolution of December 18, 1996, are diametrically opposed, particularly with respect to their operational definitions of Ebonics.

Again, Oakland had declared Ebonics to be "a language other than English," whereas the LSA stated that Ebonics is identical to "African American vernacular English." Most journalists who reported on Ebonics were apparently unaware of these facts. Combinations of poorly chosen phrases in the original Oakland resolutions were, in my opinion, having detrimental social consequences. Yes, some African Americans were absolutely thrilled by the media spotlight and the opportunity to flaunt linguistic and educational conventions, but other black people were equally outspoken regarding their anger, shame, and sense of betrayal (see chapters 8 and 9).

Prior to January 15, 1997, Oakland educators remained steadfast in their unwavering support of the original resolutions and supporting policy statement. However, on January 15, at a special meeting of the Oakland school board, a revised version of the controversial resolutions was passed. The texts of both resolutions are provided here for comparative purposes.

RESOLUTION OF THE
BOARD OF EDUCATION
ADOPTING THE REPORT AND RECOMMENDATIONS
OF THE AFRICAN AMERICAN TASK FORCE:
A POLICY STATEMENT
AND
DIRECTING THE SUPERINTENDENT OF SCHOOLS
TO DEVISE A PROGRAM TO IMPROVE THE
ENGLISH LANGUAGE ACQUISITION AND APPLICATION
SKILLS
OF AFRICAN-AMERICAN STUDENTS

No. 9697-0063

WHEREAS, numerous validated scholarly studies demonstrate that African American students as a part of their culture and history as African people possess and utilize a language described in various scholarly approaches as "Ebonics" (literally "Black sounds") or "Pan-African Communication Behaviors" or African Language Systems"; and

ORIGINAL TEXT
OF THE DECEMBER
RESOLUTION

REVISED TEXT
OF THE JANUARY
RESOLUTION

WHEREAS, these studies have also demonstrated that African Language
Systems are genetically based and not a dialect of English; and

[*WHEREAS, These studies have also demonstrated that African Language
Systems* have origins in West and Niger-Congo language and are not merely dialects of English; *and*]

WHEREAS, these studies demonstrate that such West and Niger-Congo African languages have been officially recognized and addressed in the mainstream public educational community as worthy of study, understanding or application of its principles,

[*WHEREAS, these studies demonstrate that such West and Niger-Congo African languages have been* (____) *recognized and addressed in the* (____) (____) *educational community as worthy of study, understanding* and *application of their principles,*

laws and structures for the benefit of African-American students both in terms of positive appreciation of the language and these students' acquisition and mastery of English language skills; and

WHEREAS, such recognition by scholars has given rise over the past fifteen years to legislation passed by the State of California recognizing the unique language status of descendants of slaves, with such legislation being prejudicially and unconstitutionally vetoed repeatedly by various California state governors; and

WHEREAS, judicial cases in states other than California have recognized the unique language stature of African-American pupils, and such recognition by courts has resulted in court-mandated educational programs which have substantially benefited African American children in the interest of vindicating their equal protection of the law rights under the Fourteenth Amendment to the United States Constitution; and

WHEREAS, the Federal Bilingual Education Act (20 U.S.C. 1402 *et. seq.*) mandates that local educational agencies "build their capacities to establish, implement and sustain programs of instruction for children and youth of limited English proficiency," and

WHEREAS, the interests of the Oakland Unified School District in providing equal opportunities for all of its students dictate limited English proficient educational programs recognizing the English language acquisition and improvement skills of African-American students are as fundamental as is

application of bilingual education principles for others whose primary languages are other than English;	*application of bilingual or second language learner principles for others whose primary languages are other than English. Primary languages are the language patterns children bring to school; and]*
and	

WHEREAS, the standardized tests and grade scores of African-American students in reading and language arts skills measuring their application of English skills are substantially below state and national norms and that such deficiencies will be remedied by application of a program featuring

African Language Systems principles in instructing African-American children both in their primary language and in English; and	*African Language Systems principles to move students from the language patterns they bring to school to English proficiency; and*

WHEREAS, standardized tests and grade scores will be remedied by application of a program with teachers and

aides who are certified in the methodology of featuring African Language Systems principles in instructing African-American children both in their primary language and in English.	*instructional assistants who are certified in the methodology of featuring African Language Systems principles used to transition students from the language patterns they bring to school to English.*

The certified teachers of these students will be provided incentives including, but not limited to salary differentials;

NOW, THEREFORE, BE IT RESOLVED that the Board of Education officially recognized the existence, and the cultural and historic bases of West and Niger-Congo African Language Systems, and each language as the predominantly primary language of

African-American students; and	*many African-American students;*

BE IT FURTHER RESOLVED that the Board of Education hereby adopts the report, recommendations and attached policy Statement of the District's African-American Task Force on the language stature of African-American speech; and

BE IT FURTHER RESOLVED that the Superintendent in conjunction with her staff shall immediately devise and implement

the best possible academic program for imparting instruction to African-American students in their primary language for the combined purposes of maintaining the	*the best possible academic program for (_____) the*
	combined purposes of facilitating the acquisition and mastery of English language skills, while respect-
legitimacy and richness of such	*ing and embracing the legitimacy and richness of the language pat-*
language whether it is known	*terns whether they are known*

as "Ebonics," "African Language Systems," "Pan-African Communication Behaviors" or other description, and to facilitate their acquisition and mastery of English language skills; and

BE IT FURTHER RESOLVED that the Board of Education hereby commits to earmark District general and special funding as is reasonably necessary and appropriate to enable the Superintendent and her staff to accomplish the foregoing; and

BE IT FURTHER RESOLVED that the Superintendent and her staff shall utilize the input of the entire Oakland educational community as well as state and federal scholarly and educational input in devising such a program; and

BE IT FURTHER RESOLVED that periodic reports on the progress of the creation and implementation of such an education program shall be made to the Board of Education at least once per month commencing at the Board meeting on December 18, 1996.
[*sic*]
I hereby certify that the foregoing is a full, true and correct copy of a resolution passed at a Regular [*Special*] Meeting of the Board of Ed-

ucation of the Oakland Unified School District held December 18, 1996. [*January 15, 1997.*]

- -

Secretary of the Board of Education

As both a linguist and an African American I greatly welcomed Oakland's revised resolution, and some of the most important changes are noteworthy. To me the most significant change is the essential concession that Ebonics is "not merely a dialect of English," which is quite different from claims that Ebonics is not an English dialect. The former includes Ebonics within the English speech community; the latter excludes Ebonics from the English language. There are direct policy implications associated with this change, which could explain why the revised proposal still refers to African American students as "second language learners." Such linguistic representation would include African Americans with other students "whose primary languages are other than English."

Some apparent contradictions remain within the revised Oakland resolution, but previous references to Ebonics as "genetically based" or that "such West and Niger-Congo African languages have been officially recognized and addressed in the mainstream public" have been dropped. However many controversial assertions still prevail.

Prior to the revised January 15 resolution, Oakland's Ebonics definition and that contained within the LSA resolution were diametrically opposed. In my opinion neither the Oakland nor the LSA resolutions were adequate.

Weinreich (1953) amplifies the linguist's definitional dilemma:

> [I]t is immaterial whether the two systems are "languages," "dialects of the same language," or "varieties of the same dialect." The greater the difference between the systems, i.e., the more numerous the mutually exclusive forms and patterns in each, the greater is the learning problem and the potential area of interference.

My belief that African American English is a dialect of English, and not a separate language, is based on the preceding observation—namely, the "mutually exclusive forms and patterns in each (i.e., Ebonics and standard English) are educationally significant but insufficient to justify classification as a language other than English. Also, if one concedes that Ebonics is not English, should we then make another distinction between "standard Ebonics" and "nonstandard Ebonics," and, if so, on what basis would we determine the standard form of the language derived from American slavery? I know of no such designation, but language educators routinely draw on such fundamental distinctions for instructional purposes.

I too wish that Oakland educators had specified the need for standard English proficiency rather than their more global reference to "English proficiency." The latter strikes me as an attempt to maintain linguistic and educational analogies to English language learners for whom Title VII funds are now allocated. This interpretation would, of course, conflict with assertions that the Oakland school board "never intended to ask for bilingual funds," which is further complicated by Applebome's (1997b) report that "Oakland officials said they expected most of the cost of the new policy to come from reallocating existing financing, but they left open the possibility of apply for Title 7 money." But the preliminary response from Washington balked at the proposed bilingual interpretation of Ebonics, "a spokesman [sic] said Federal law specifically [sic] viewed black English as a form of English, not a separate language eligible for Title VII money."

Legislative Lament

Politicians weren't far behind the press in hot pursuit of Ebonics. Although spokespersons from the U.S. Department of Education fired some early warning shots across the Ebonics bow, categorically rejecting any suggestion that African Americans speak a foreign language, Secretary Richard Riley was the first national figure to officially reject assertions that Ebonics is anything other than an English dialect. On December 24, 1996, only six days after the Oakland school board passed its controversial resolution, Secretary Riley exclaimed, "The Administration's policy is that Ebonics is a nonstandard form of English and not a foreign language" (*New York Times*, Dec. 24, 1996, p. A22).

By then Oakland had hired a public relations firm. The board was no longer coy about its unfulfilled Title VII aspirations; the board simply denied any such allegations. From that point forward few politicians voiced support for Oakland, although there were noteworthy exceptions. Despite Oakland's statements to the contrary, Secretary Riley was unwilling to equate Ebonics with other foreign languages that are eligible for Title VII. Had he done otherwise, this story would have turned out quite differently; under that alternative scenario, equating Ebonics with languages other than English, countless school districts from across the country would have quickly lined up at the federal Title VII trough, each claiming circumstances comparable with Oakland's, along with equally strong intent to promote standard English fluency among their own Ebonics-speaking students.

When Secretary Riley said that "elevating black English to the status of a language is not the way to raise standards of achievement in our schools and for our students," he simultaneously dashed any hope that Oakland's resolutions would ever be honored or viewed as educationally visionary. Beyond any linguistic or educational displeasure that Riley displayed publicly lie the nuts-and-bolts policy procedures that apply specifically to Title VII. Title VII funding is for students who do not speak English; that's it in a nutshell. African Americans are not considered language-minority students under this definition. Through Oakland's interpretation of Ebonics as a non-English language, however, African American students would be similar to other Title VII students. As legislative tides drifted away from affirmative action, Oakland's Ebonics resolutions swam against those currents into a torrent of hostile public opinion. Once publicized, Oakland's linguistic assertions came under closer media scrutiny, and its educational policies were vociferously challenged from both sides of the political spectrum, yielding the scorn, racism, ridicule, and political vilification that soon became the constant traveling companions of Ebonics.

The vast majority of poor school districts that teach substantial numbers of black students would no doubt welcome more support to bolster standard English proficiency; however, because federal definitions of language-minority students are delineated so as to exclude nonstandard English, African American students for whom standard English is not native continue to be ignored by federal educational language policies. Oakland was threatening to reslice the Title VII pie, thereby invoking Secretary Riley's prompt regulatory restraint.

Those who speak English in America with a distinctive accent should pray that it's one that most Americans find appealing—otherwise some will inevitably ridicule their speech. The public outrage sparked by Ebonics highlights this linguistic reality and the anger was stimulated by the pervasive misconception that students and teachers were going to be taught Ebonics at the taxpayers' expense.

Most taxpayers cringed at the prospect that Ebonics could ever be taken seriously—linguistically, educationally, or otherwise. Many people, from different racial backgrounds, were angered by the racial divisions and innuendo that saturated most Afrocentric Ebonics definitions. But negative public opinion could not negate the regulatory realities that Secretary Riley faced: He realized that statutory classification of Ebonics as a foreign language had the potential to lead to legal, political, and educational entanglements that might easily spin out of control.

Few people fully understand how federal educational programs work, but Title VII differs significantly from other federal educational funding (e.g., it's not an entitlement). Students don't automatically get Title VII funds simply because English isn't their mother tongue. They must attend a school or a school district that has made a formal grant application to Washington. Other federal educational funding is coordinated collaboratively with the states, but Title VII skips over the state departments of education and goes directly to schools and school districts from the U.S. Department of Education.

The prospect of thousands of Ebonics requests for Title VII funds would not be welcomed by either Democrats or Republicans, if for no other reason than budgetary considerations. Corresponding "political costs" are even more difficult to calculate in a socially charged public atmosphere in which education, language, race, and affirmative action are simultaneously in play. I therefore presume that Secretary Riley, aware that Title VII applications could soon arrive on his doorstep, did everything he could to keep the "Oakland Ebonics express" from ever leaving the station. From the standpoint of educational policy, then, the difference between a dialect and a language is substantial; it's the difference between access to Title VII funding or not.

Alameda County is among the most linguistically diverse of any in California, and Oakland schools serve students from many different linguistic backgrounds. In part, it was the result of its extensive experience teaching language-minority students that Oakland—in advance of school districts that are comparatively less diverse—attempted to define Ebonics in harmony with Title VII regulations.

I would be among the first to acknowledge the worthiness of effective educational programs to enhance student literacy and corresponding standard English proficiency, but to do so by reinventing linguistic history is not only misleading but denies linguistic reality in wrongful subordination to federal educational regulations that are considerably outdated and inadequate.

Secretary Riley did not anticipate Ebonics; rather, he reacted to it as a potential political crisis, and by rejecting black access to Title VII he nipped similar prospects in the bud, all in the name of maintaining high academic standards. I, for one, fully expected the other shoe to drop; namely, would Secretary Riley offer positive solutions to this specific educational problem: What should teachers do to advance black standard English proficiency? One appropriate response would have been to propose a plan to address the linguistic consequences of slavery in pursuit of educational parity. But to do that would acknowledge that students who do not learn standard English natively are not competing on an even educational playing field, having begun their formal education at a considerable linguistic disadvantage.

Returning to the language of American slave descendants, there are two ways to handle revising linguistic classifications for minority students: One might argue (as I have) that current classifications are too restrictive (Baugh 1998), or one might argue (as Oakland did) that African Americans, by way of their Ebonic linguistic inheritance, already meet existing criteria for LEP. Neither approach has made any real headway because the prevailing political climate is such that most citizens link standard English to intelligence and personal discipline. Linguistic Darwinism prevails throughout the nation. Many Americans no longer interpret linguistic and cognitive matters in overtly racial terms; they assume that those who are sufficiently intelligent and disciplined enough to employ standard English will do so. Linguistic stereotypes offer the illusion of egalitarianism because they claim to be free of any racial taint or bias. The argument that sustains them asserts that all people are free to speak in any manner they choose. According to these stereotypes, those who choose to "speak properly" have always been considered to be more intelligent than those who "speak badly."

In the United States, where English is used for the vast majority of institutionalized discourse, standard American English fluency is an economic asset (Baugh 1996; Coulmas 1992). Fluent standard English speakers tend to hold the most influential positions of political and economic power in the nation, and those who lack standard English fluency rarely attain comparable social stature in society. This recognition helps to account for the anti-Ebonics outcry that followed news of Oakland's Ebonics assertions.

In an effort to satiate the growing public appetite for Ebonics retribution, politicians from various political persuasions submitted legislation to squash Ebonics as quickly as possible. Representative Peter T. King (R-N.Y.), perhaps best known for dubbing Speaker Newt Gingrich "political roadkill," was first among them on January 14, 1997, when he drafted a resolution that said in part:

> Whereas "Ebonics" is not a legitimate language: Now, therefore, be it Resolved, that it is the sense of the House of Representatives that no Federal funds should be used to pay for or support any program that is based upon the premise that "Ebonics" is a legitimate language.

This resolution attracted few cosponsors, and was sent to committee just as the Ebonics controversy began fading from public attention. There are some constitutional problems associated with the wording of King's bill, and many congressional members have stated publicly and privately that they found the Ebonics controversy to be a racially divisive social distraction that only aggravated tender racial wounds.

Shortly thereafter, on January 23, 1997, Senator Arlen Specter (R-Pa.) who then chaired the Senate subcommittee on Labor, Health, Human Services, and Education, convened Ebonics hearings, which he opened on an empathic note. He began by recounting his own linguistic heritage as the child of Jewish immigrants who spoke Yiddish in their home, and of an older brother, a fluent Yiddish speaker, who was the victim of anti-Semitic linguistic discrimination. His words were a moving testament to the legacy of linguistic diversity that is such an integral historical component of American culture, and it was clear at the outset that Senator Specter had not prejudged Oakland educators or Ebonics.

Such was not the case for Senator Lauch Faircloth (R-N.C.), who spoke next at the hearings; he decried the politics of race and their Ebonic surrogates as one of the most "absurd" examples of extreme "political correctness" that he had ever encountered. As a white male Republican senator from North Carolina who speaks with a strong and distinctive southern accent, his views could not have been more symbolically or diametrically opposed to those of Representative Maxine

Waters (D-Cal.), an African American woman who, at the time of the hearing, served as chair of the Congressional Black Caucus. She responded directly to Senator Faircloth, expressing her opposition to his statement and affirming her understanding of the Oakland school board's intention to teach standard English, not Ebonics, to African American students enrolled in that district.

The contrasting opinions expressed by these federal legislators could not have been more striking; the opponent of Ebonics being white, male, Southern, and conservative and the proponent of teaching standard English to black students being black, female, and more liberal. As should be the case in the halls of a democratic Congress, they spoke not only for themselves but also for their constituents. Having first heard from federal political representatives, the hearings shifted to comments from Oakland educators and an Oakland high school senior of considerable academic distinction.

They took their seats and were introduced. The group included Dr. Carolyn Getridge, former superintendent of the school district, and two members of the Oakland school board, along with a member of the district's African American task force who also worked closely with teachers involved in the SEP program. Dr. Getridge began, seeking to clarify the goals of the school district, stating that references to Ebonics in the district's resolutions were not intended to endorse a particular linguistic point of view. She acknowledged that it was her goal and intention to provide the best possible education to students within her district. She clearly stated that it was not the districts intention to seek federal bilingual education funding, while pointing out that some individual schools within the district had used Title I funding for their SEP programs. During follow-up questions Senator Specter asked if Dr. Getridge was aware of the pending legislation from Representative Peter King that would restrict any federal funding for programs based on Ebonics. She responded that based on her understanding of the relevant statutes, King could not impose such a law because it would contradict provisions in the revised 1994 Equal Educational Opportunity Act, which deregulated many federal educational programs in favor of greater local educational jurisdiction, especially regarding the education of children from low-income backgrounds.

Toni Cook, the member of the school board who chaired Oakland's African American task force, reported that the task force was created at the behest of the board to help alter the dismal record of academic performance of so many of the African American students who were currently and previously enrolled in the district (see chapter 4). Like many other urban school districts serving large numbers of low-income students of color, Oakland was attempting to find alternative strategies to the established trends of educational failure that it found unacceptable. Additional remarks by Oakland's representatives painted a picture of a school district under siege.

Jean Quan, president of the school board, in direct response to a question from Senator Specter, described the dilemma that Oakland educators typically face. After a brief aside regarding concerns about the potential inadequacy of existing bilingual education funding for traditional students with LEP, she turned to the reality in Oakland classrooms, exclaiming that it was difficult for Oakland's teachers to offer special language instruction to language-minority students supported by Title VII in various classes when they occupy the same classrooms with African American students who are also in need of special linguistic education and for whom no provision is made under federal law. Her testimony was powerful and convincing, especially as she spoke with considerable knowledge of the educational plight of traditional language-minority students.

The next men to testify were highly critical of Ebonics, or any suggestion that educational programs be derived from it. The first was an African American minister who quoted references to scripture in his denouncement of "bad English" and "slang" as having no place in educational contexts. He talked about his own background, as one of several poor children in a family whose parents had only been able to complete a small portion of an elementary education. His parents were demanding, he said, having high expectations and aspirations for all their children. They did not tolerate "bad language," nor did they accept anything less than their children's best possible efforts.

Although his comments were inspired, he portrayed the Oakland educational venture as one that had acquiesced to lower academic standards. He did not place entire blame for student failure at the feet of the school district but spoke instead of the need for "a holistic approach" that would engage the entire community, including the involvement of churches to support educational efforts with extracurricular programs. He also appealed directly to the Senate for additional flexibility in educational funding that would make such church participation more feasible.

Despite obvious good intentions, his constant references to bad English, broken English, and street slang were somewhat misplaced; yes, these are the prevailing stereotypes about the vernacular speech of American slave descendants, but those like this minister and Representative King who equate Ebonics with ungrammatical English or nonstandard English are being overly simplistic and are therefore unlikely to advance black students toward greater standard English proficiency.

Such was the case for the next speaker, a conservative African American radio talk show host who had previously worked on Capitol Hill for Senator Strom Thurmond. He too castigated the Oakland school board, but his opposition was based on numerous linguistic stereotypes and other misconceptions. He told of being taught French by a teacher who never used English, although he and his fellow students were all native speakers of English. I suspect he failed to realize that he was inadvertently lending credence to the extreme interpretation of Ebonics as a foreign language. Be that as it may, most of his linguistic analogies, which devalued Ebonics and the Oakland school board policies, were derived from his own experience in learning French as a second language. He also made some medical analogies, stating that a physician need not contract a disease to learn how to cure it.

Senator Specter then asked both speakers if they had heard the previous testimony from the Oakland representatives, and if either speaker objected to their plans to teach standard English. Their essential objection remained over the relative utility—or lack thereof—of making any reference whatsoever to the home language of African American students. Because both speakers felt, quite adamantly, that black English was simply bad English and wrong, they felt it had no place in school. The gentleman who had learned French from a teacher who never used any English referred again to his own bilingual education as a model for the school district. He felt that Oakland educators could better serve their students by avoiding any use or reference to nonstandard English, or Ebonics. The stage was then set to hear from academic scholars.

Four scholars spoke before the Senate on January 23, 1997, including Michael Casserly, Executive Director of the Council of the Great City Schools. He was armed with comparative data about African

American students from across the country, and pointed to a combination of evidence that explained some of the substantial gaps in academic performance between black and white students. He also took time to identify some existing programs that were attempting to improve standard English proficiency among African American students.

His remarks complemented those of Orlando Taylor, dean of graduate studies at Howard University, and former dean of Howard's College of Communication. Taylor was one of the participants in the 1973 St. Louis conference where the term "Ebonics" was born (see chapter 2). He has been a leading figure in studies of black speech and communication in linguistics, speech pathology, communication, and education ever since receiving his doctorate from the University of Michigan in 1966. He also participated in a 1992 conference at Stanford University on "African American English in Schools and Society," and, along with me, participated in a 1996 conference sponsored by Oakland's SEP program.

He offered pragmatic words of caution and advice that set a positive tone. At the outset he stressed linguistic diversity among African Americans, thereby circumventing the controversial genetic phrasing that had been a major source of public consternation among blacks and nonblacks who scoffed at the educational legitimacy of Oakland's efforts. In reference to Ebonics, Taylor noted that it is "a learned, social dialect that is at variance with standard American English and one that is spoken by many—but certainly by no means all—African Americans." He went on to observe that "far too many African American children have not acquired sufficient proficiency in standard English to facilitate academic success and career mobility." Similar to the resolution passed by the LSA (see appendix A), Taylor used a series of terms for African American language that implied synonymity: "[T]hese children speak as their primary language system a rule governed social dialect of English referred to variously as Ebonics, African American English, Black English, Black English Vernacular, African American Language Systems, etc." However, unlike the resolution unanimously adopted by linguists in attendance at the 1997 annual meeting of the LSA, Taylor did not equivocate on the difference between a dialect and a language, nor did he deny that Ebonics is English: "This variety of English, as other nonstandard English dialects, has often been stigmatized by the mainstream society."

He also observed another important point that has direct bearing on educational policies and related regulations, namely, that "African American children are not the only children who come to school speaking a non-standard or regional social dialect." I will return to this point momentarily, because the Ebonics debate—in my opinion—has focused too narrowly on the language of black students while obscuring the larger educational picture regarding students from other racial backgrounds who also have limited standard English proficiency. The essence of Taylor's advice was captured nicely when he observed that "these academic pursuits should not—indeed must not—cause us to blur our sights on the larger goal of how to teach standard English to all of our nation's children and yet celebrate their diversity and their ability to communicate effectively in a variety of settings."

The hearing then turned to William Labov, an internationally acclaimed leader in the field of sociolinguistics, a member of the National Academy of Science, and former president of the LSA. Labov was among the first linguists to conduct extensive and exhaustive analyses of African American speech patterns, beginning in 1966 when he examined the relationship between reading, or the lack of it, and peer group status and linguistic behavior among socially diverse minority teens in Harlem. His research, "The Logic of Nonstandard English," was the single most important article ever written that debunked the pervasive linguistic fallacies associated with the cognitive-deficit hypotheses embodied in the work of Jensen (1969) and Shockley (1972), along with others who were equally misguided and linguistically uninformed about the language of black children.

With a combination of candor and diplomacy, Labov began by emphasizing the following:

> [The international origins of] "Ebonics", which is our main focus here, has been used to suggest that there is a language, or features of language, that are common to all people of African ancestry, whether they live in Africa, Brazil, or the United States. Linguists who have published studies of the African American community have not used this term, but refer instead to African American English, or Black English, meaning all the ways that the English language is used by African Americans in this country.

Having clarified some of the confusion over the terminology, Labov then reiterated Taylor's point:

[T]his African American Vernacular English is a dialect of English, which shares most of the grammar and vocabulary with other dialects of English. But it is distinctly different in many ways, and more different from standard English than any other dialect spoken in continental North America. It is not a set of slang words, or a random set of grammatical mistakes, but a well formed set of rules of grammar and pronunciation that is capable of conveying complex logic and reasoning.

Labov then outlined the history of the relevant linguistic research, as well as his prior participation in the 1979 black English trial, which, was won on behalf of the African American plaintiffs who brought suit against the defendant school district for not providing suitable education to help them obtain standard English proficiency. His representation of corresponding linguistic facts, including evidence pertaining to "the divergence hypothesis" that vernacular black English and standard English are growing apart, rather than converging, is much more controversial among professional linguists than was conveyed during the Senate hearings. However, Labov identified "the heart of the controversy," to which Senator Specter drew additional attention:

There are two major points of view taken by educators. One view is that any recognition of a nonstandard language as a legitimate means of expression will only confuse children, and reinforce their tendency to use it instead of standard English. The other is that children learn most rapidly in their home language, and that they can benefit in both motivation and achievement by getting a head start in learning to read and write in this way. Both of these are honestly held and deserve a fair hearing.

At the conclusion of the academic testimony Senator Specter focused on these trends and asked Labov to offer his best advice on which trend to follow. Citing the work of Canadian scholars, who studied bilingual acquisition from native French to English, Labov argued that there was considerable evidence that the second approach had met with considerable success elsewhere. During a radio interview on National Public Radio, Labov was even more explicit. He argued that educators who seek to expunge vernacular African American English from their classrooms do a disservice to students by teaching techniques that overtly or implicitly deny the child use of his or her home language while gaining standard English proficiency. Labov emphasized that he was not an educator but it was apparent to him from many sources of evidence that prevailing educational techniques for most African American students were simply not working, and that other procedures should be tested before being discarded without "a fair trial."

The last scholar to speak was Robert L. Williams, professor emeritus from Washington University in St. Louis and the creator of the term "Ebonics," which he defined as "the linguistic and paralinguistic features which on a concentric continuum represent the communicative competence of the West African, Caribbean, and United States slave descendent of African origin" (1975:V). Williams characterized the "concentric continuum" in historical linguistic terms:

> "Concentric continuum" describes the expanse of black language in its continuously overlapping development as a function of the influences by which it has been affected. For example, a slave might have been influenced by Portuguese, and later English, and then French, and later still, Portuguese in an American setting. From each of these languages, the black slave assumed some linguistic skills which have been used as the need arose: the African's own language added to the complexity of the speech [*sic*] (s)he ultimately spoke." (1975:vi)

As repeated throughout this book, the original Ebonics definition did not refer exclusively to what we linguists call African American vernacular English or black vernacular English; rather, it was far more comprehensive. In much the same manner that Chomsky's (1965) notion of "universal grammar" exceeds the bounds of any single language or group of languages, so too did the original definition of Ebonics encompass all the languages that were in contact as a result of the African slave trade. This would, of course, include many indigenous African and European languages in contact, as described by Williams's concentric continuum.

Taking a different tack from either Taylor or Labov, Williams offered an autobiographical sketch of his own life, having attended high school in Little Rock, Arkansas, where he earned an IQ test score of 82, only to later defy the educational odds and graduate cum laude from Philander Smith College in 1953. He then described his 1970 research resulting in the development of the BITCH, which showed that African Americans performed better on a test that contained items that were culturally familiar. Williams is not a linguist, and many of the translations he wrote in *Ebonics* (1975) are not exclusive to African Americans (see chapter 2). This was again confirmed during his Senate testimony where he reproduced the examples that served as the basis for his original research and the primordial formulation of Ebonics.

Williams concluded his testimony by endorsing the cross-cultural reading program, "Bridge," developed by Gary Simpkins and Grace Holt (1977), which is based on the recognition that students who speak African American vernacular English must gradually learn standard English norms if they hope to succeed academically. The program was controversial for some of the very reasons indicated during Labov's testimony, namely, the authors intentionally utilize African American English in their educational materials. Many educators objected to such a practice claiming it would increase reliance on the nonstandard vernacular at the expense of more rapid development of standard English. But Williams, Labov, and others have defended the educational philosophy behind the Bridge program because it begins by using the vernacular language that is native to many black students.

During follow-up questions with Senator Specter, Williams stressed the elastic nature of Ebonics, claiming he used it with considerable regularity. These exchanges evoked smiles and occasional laughter in the otherwise somber chamber, but Senator Specter asked for clarification. He wanted to know about the transition to standard English: "How long will it take?" This question is often the identical question that is asked by both proponents and detractors of bilingual education, and Williams—much like advocates of bilingual education—was unable to specify a definitive timetable for the transition from Ebonics to standard English.

The Senate hearings ended on a conciliatory note. Senator Specter thanked all present for attending, and also stated that he fully expected to convene one or more hearings with other witnesses who had not yet had an opportunity to testify. However, as media attention began to diminish, so too did the political fireworks that had been ignited in Oakland, and in the end no such hearings were convened.

While federal officials were contemplating their course of action with reference to Ebonics, several state politicians had already submitted anti-Ebonics legislation with the explicit intention of precluding any educational effort to embrace Ebonics. That flurry of state legislative activity was also short-winded and shortsighted. Some states, such as Texas (see appendix B), took an enlightened approach, calling for additional research and information to resolve educational problems confronting African American students. Other states, including California, where Ebonics had been incubating through the SEP program, held politically contentious hearings that sputtered as soon as African American Ebonics detractors accused members of the California legislature of racially motivated political opportunism at the expense of California's black students. California's H.B. 205 (see appendix C) went down to defeat in committee, partially because it too had badly misrepresented the linguistic legacy of American slavery and its detrimental impact on the educational advancement of the vast majority of African American students who—despite some encouraging signs of educational improvement—still lag too far behind their white peers.

Legal Implications

At the height of the Ebonics controversy few Americans were able to dispassionately step back and realize that Oakland was trapped between conflicting state and federal regulations. California's SEP program acknowledged the fact that many African American students could be considered language-minority students, whereas corresponding federal statutes excluded African Americans from comparable language-minority classification. The technical, indeed legal, discrepancy lies between the essential distinction between standard English proficiency (which was Oakland's goal) and English proficiency (as specified in federal statutes). Although one would presume that all native English speakers acquire English proficiency, many native English speakers never acquire standard English proficiency.

What level of linguistic proficiency is needed for academic success? Is it merely English proficiency, as implied by Title VII, or is it standard English proficiency, as suggested by Oakland educators during their Senate testimony? Oakland educators faced another dilemma. They had assumed a leading role among their peers within California's SEP programs, which existed in seventeen school districts throughout the state.

Under federal regulations, however, no educational provisions are made for speakers of nonstandard English, with one noticeable exception: native Hawaiians. Native Hawaiians were provided with special federal categorical funding for bidialectal education that acknowledges the educational constraints derived from nonstandard Hawaiian pidgin English (HPE).

In sharp contrast to the Ebonics controversy, it has been politically and economically feasible to consider a small bidialectal linguistic enrichment program in Hawaii, isolated from the mainland; however, there are striking historical linguistic parallels between the creation of HPE and the genesis of slavery-induced nonstandard African American English. There are striking historical differences as well: English engulfed native Hawaiians, whereas enslaved Africans were ingested into Southern American English, albeit as human chattel denied any inalienable rights.

From a linguistic point of view slavery has yet to be fully overcome, because American slave descendants have blended more slowly into the melting pot than have immigrants with lighter shades of skin. Federal educational policies have ignored helping African American students toward greater standard English proficiency. Again, most Americans view acquiring such proficiency as a matter of personal free will, having little if anything to do with racial background. But African American English is unique among America's nonstandard English dialects; it is the only one born of slavery and the educational restraints imposed by slavery. No reasonable person can deny that the legacy of racially segregated education has had negative social consequences for the majority of American slave descendants. Oakland's Ebonics strategy never rose to the ultimate test of a court challenge, and so the legal status of African American English (and perhaps other nonstandard English dialects) remains unresolved.

The Ebonics episode is cast in the shadow of two Supreme Court rulings: *Brown v. Board of Education* (1954) is, of course, the paramount ruling concerning racially segregated public education, resulting in the holding that segregated educational facilities were "separate and unequal." *Lau v. Nichols* (1974) is the ruling that asserts the rights of language-minority students, implying that students for whom English is not native define that group; again, HPE is an important statutory exception. Oakland educators, having been leaders in the SEP program to bolster standard English among black students, found themselves in a fierce game of regulatory ping-pong between contradictory federal and California definitions of African Americans as legitimate or illegitimate language-minority students. Oakland operated on the SEP assumption that many African American students should be classified as language-minority students, and the emergence of Afrocentric Ebonics definitions tended to reinforce that view.

In the wake of the "black English trial," in 1979, California's state board of education adopted a policy for SEP, titled "Black Language: Proficiency in Standard English for Speakers of Black Language." We shall consider the content of this policy momentarily. The term "Black Language" is not one we linguists employ. Indeed, the use of such a term officially opened the door to the extreme Afrocentric interpretations of Ebonics that influenced Oakland's infamous resolutions in the first place.

Had the California State Board of Education used the term "Black English" rather than "Black Language," much of the current confusion over Ebonics might have been avoided. But the term "Black Language" could indeed be interpreted to apply to all people of African ancestry, regardless of linguistic background. Do Ibo and Bantu speakers and speakers of Haitian Creole also fall within California's undefined reference to "Black Language"? From both a legal and linguistic point of view, the use of the term "Black Language" placed California's SEP policy on a treacherously weak foundation from the outset. By forcing matters of race and language together, California's State Board of Education inadvertently set Oakland on a collision course with Secretary Riley, at the same time that it inadvertently opened the door to ideologically driven interpretations of linguistic history.

Proponents of Ebonics, which for some time included leaders of Oakland's SEP program, advanced the tenuous linguistic interpretation that Ebonics is not English. However, if African Americans do not speak English, presumably we would be covered under the *Lau* ruling and should be eligible for Title VII, as suggested in Oakland's first resolution. *Brown* dealt with matters of educational inequities based on racial heritage and never focused on linguistic matters in their own right. It was not until 1979, during the "black English trial," that a federal court ruled on a case in which African American race, education, and language were conjoined. Senator Specter, an attorney by profession, observed that the

African American plaintiffs won the black English case against the defendant school district, which had previously made no provision to help its African American students master standard English.

California state educators who followed the black English trial observed the ruling in favor of the plaintiffs and consequently developed the SEP program to ward off the prospect of similar litigation from African Americans in California, who—prior to the establishment of the SEP program—could have easily brought similar suits against school districts throughout the state. It's important to reemphasize that the African American plaintiffs won their case. Judge Charles Joiner, who presided over the black English trial, ultimately ruled in favor of the black plaintiffs, observing that the defendant school district demanded standard English proficiency of African American students but made no provision in teacher education or ensuing student instruction to acknowledge the legitimate language barriers imposed by the plaintiff's native nonstandard vernacular English.

Although California state educators responded to Judge Joiner's ruling by creating the SEP program, the defendant school district did not appeal his decision. Rather, the district submitted a plan to enhance teacher education, and although this resolved the immediate problem for Judge Joiner and his federal district court, it did not have the national clout of *Brown* or *Lau v. Nichols*. To have a stronger, more pervasive effect, it needed to be appealed to a higher court with broader jurisdiction, but that was never done. Consequently, while the federal government didn't budge on this issue, California's state board of education scrambled to introduce educational programs for black students to increase their standard English proficiency under the SEP program. Some of the most salient legal precedents are found in *Plessy v. Ferguson* (1896), which affirmed that slaves had no legal rights. *Sweatt v. Painter* (1950) and *McClaurin v. Oklahoma* (1950) focused on unequal graduate education for blacks within a law school and a graduate school respectively. *Brown* dealt with racially segregated K–12 public education. Each of the preceding cases concentrated on unequal treatment of African Americans. *Lau v. Nichols* dealt with the education and definition of language-minority students, excluding African Americans. Again, the black English trial brought African American race, education, and English together for the first time within the context of litigation central to the academic welfare and advancement of African American students.

The content of California's standard English proficiency program is most informative at this juncture, because it came under vociferous attack in California's Senate Bill 205, written by Senator Haynes, who appeared hell-bent to eliminate SEP and Ebonics with a single blow. His effort eventually fizzled due to a combination of linguistic misinformation and personalized political attacks. But the central object of his attention was the policy titled "Proficiency in Standard English for speakers of Black Language":

CALIFORNIA STATE BOARD OF EDUCATION

Policy Adopted 2/81

Subject: Black Language: Proficiency in Standard English for Speakers of Black Language

The State Board of Education and the State Department of Education, realizing that there is a need to provide for proficiency in English for California students who are speakers of Black language, and to provide equal educational opportunities for these students, do hereby recognize:

(a) that oral language development is a key strategy which facilitates learning to achieve in reading and in other academic areas

(b) that structured oral language practice in standard English should be provided on an ongoing basis

(c) that oral language development should be emphasized during the teaching of reading and writing

(d) that special program strategies are required to address the needs of speakers of Black language

(e) that staff development should be provided for policy makers, administrators, instructional personnel and other responsible persons

(f) that parents and the general public should be informed of implications of educational strategies to address the linguistic needs of Black students

(g) that this effort to improve proficiency in standard English for speakers of Black language is NOT: (1) a program for students to be taught to speak Black language; (2) a program for teachers to learn to speak Black language; (3) a program requiring materials in textbooks to be written in Black language.

Therefore, the State Board of Education and the State Department of Education, with the adoption of this policy statement, provide direction and leadership to the districts and schools of the State of California in the development and refinement of proficiency in English programs for speakers of Black language. The State Board of Education hereby declares:

(a) that school districts should develop and implement strategies to increase proficiency in English for speakers of Black language

(b) that the State Department of Education, in cooperation with school districts, should provide for appropriate staff development for teachers, administrators and other school personnel

(c) that any existing general or categorical funds should be used to address these linguistic needs

(d) that local boards should adopt policies which specifically address the needs of speakers of Black language and facilitate the implementation of this state policy in their districts.

I consider most of the preceding educational goals to be worthy and laudable, but, again, the decision to use "Black Language" rather than "Black English" easily leads to linguistic interpretations that are inclusive of all black people—regardless of language background—and some definitions of Ebonics tout this view (Blackshire-Belay 1996). Although "Ebonics" was first coined in 1973 (see chapter 2), no reference was made to it in the 1979 black English trial or in the preceding California's "Black Language" policy, given in full in the preceding extract. However, in the view of Senator Haynes and his supporters, SEP had spawned Ebonics. That interpretation is misleading, and S.B. 205 went to extraordinary lengths to avoid any reference to "standard English," seeking instead to find synonymous surrogates that merely confused the bill's objectives.

For example, S.B. 205 portrays the SEP program as one "that explicitly directs teachers to do both of the following: (A) incorporate slang into their lesson plans, (B) teach that slang is an appropriate alternative to correct English is some situations." S.B. 205 also asserts the following:

> [C]alling their programs "Ebonics," these districts are attempting to convince students that poor communication skills are acceptable speech patterns and writing skills, and that these students cannot learn to speak correct English due to social or cultural factors outside their control. The justification for "Ebonics" instruction is the same as that used to justify separate educational institutions for African-Americans prior to the case of Brown v. Board of Education. It is the perpetuation of the "separate but equal" philosophy that has harmed race relations in this country for far too many years.

Delaine Eastin, California's state superintendent of public instruction, wrote to Senator Leroy Green, chair of California's Senate Education Committee, to oppose S.B. 205. She criticized many of the misrepresentations asserted in S.B. 205 that she found objectionable:

> We strongly oppose S.B. 205 because it misrepresents the California Department of Education's SEP program. Further, S.B. 205 takes out of context contents of the SEP handbook to politicize the issue of language acquisition by racial minority students.

Here too Superintendent Eastin evades the specificity of the SEP program for African Americans by cloaking her reservations within the broader "issue of language acquisition by racial minority students." Racial minority students are not exclusively African American, but the SEP program is only intended to serve speakers of Black Language.

Both the SEP policy statement and S.B. 205 are problematic from legal, educational, and linguistic points of view. Taking the last point first: Linguists would never use race to define a linguistic group; Black Language is therefore problematic and defies traditional language or dialect classifications. S.B. 205 uses terms such as "correct English" and "proper English" without defining them; it appears that these terms are being used as substitutes for standard English.

Had supporters of S.B. 205 gathered the necessary support to pass their bill, they would have faced the more daunting linguistic task of attempting to ensure that the "Equality in English Instruction Act" could indeed "improve linguistic or communication skills of students in low-income areas of the state [sic] with financial penalties for school districts where the skills have deteriorated, as measured by objective testing data." I know of no existing testing data suited to this task. Had S.B. 205 become California law, which it did not, school districts with large numbers of low-income students would be compelled to demonstrate "improved linguistic or communication skills"; presumably educators in middle- and upper-income school districts would not be subject to this law.

Linguists use the terms "standard" and "nonstandard" (rather than substandard) when referring to dialects within a language. Although speakers of every language share myths regarding proper or improper usage, linguists tend not to speak about "correct" or "incorrect" language. For example, most of us have been taught that the use of "ain't" is either incorrect or improper; few of us were ever told that "ain't" is grammatical but also a nonstandard colloquialism (which it is in actuality). So, why don't linguists characterize nonstandard dialects as "incorrect"? To do so would be misleading and false; ordinary speech and prescribed standards for formal linguistic usage have varied throughout recorded history.

Every major world language can be characterized in terms of a standard versus nonstandard dichotomy. This dichotomy often translates into the provincial equivalent of formal versus informal use of the language. There are incontrovertible class differences and regional differences that reinforce these impressions, and the most formal renditions of "language X" also tend to represent the formal or "proper" speech of the corresponding social elite. Unlike European languages whose standard dialects frequently derive from historical regal speech, standard American English has great regional variation (e.g., as reflected in the various accents represented by American politicians).

My questions to California's Senator Haynes, or others who prefer the term "correct English" over "standard English," are, How should we define "correct English"? And would that definition differ in any way from linguistic formulations of "standard English"? It is quite evident that Senator Haynes sought to distance his legislation from SEP, by avoiding the phrase "standard English" (which saturates the SEP regulations) in favor of "proper English" or "correct English," which—if those terms are not synonymous with "standard English"—should be clearly defined. The only justification for using the terms "correct English" or "proper English" appears to be politically motivated.

As of this writing these legal details remain in limbo, and we are likely to see them resurface again because the educational plight of most African American students remains bleak, and uninformed linguistic stereotypes about African American English (or Ebonics) also prevail. The Oakland case might have turned out differently had Oakland built its analogy around the categorical program for HPE rather than Title VII. For example, could Secretary Riley claim that HPE is not English in the same manner that he scoffed at the concept that Ebonics is not English? How can the federal government justify a worthy linguistic program to increase standard English among HPE speakers and not extend the same linguistic concerns to speakers of African American English?

A substantial portion of the answers to these complex questions lies between Judge Joiner's ruling in the black English trial, the formulation of California's SEP program, and the mushrooming influence of Afrocentric interpretations of Ebonics that infiltrated SEP programs, culminating in the contentious Ebonics resolutions that equated black children with all other language minority students (i.e., those covered by the *Lau* ruling). How, then, did this happen? What events transpired that could lead some African American scholars and educators to their controversial Ebonics conclusions?

Disparate Theoretical Foundations

Studies of African American speech are robust, and especially so in four scholarly fields:

- The Afrocentric tradition, which has given birth to Ebonics;
- Speech pathology and language disorders among African American children;
- Educational concerns regarding the language of black students; and
- Linguistic research, specializing in detailed scientific analyses of vernacular African American English.

What are some of the underlying theoretical assumptions that drive research in these related fields, and why do scholars come to disparate linguistic conclusions?

Our survey of theory in these fields begins with some alternative Afrocentric interpretations of Ebonics, beyond those previously described. Speech pathologists, educators, and linguists who specialize in African American language gradually became aware of Ebonics through contact with Afrocentric scholarship. Because there is no unequivocal definition of Ebonics, its transformation from an international construct into one pertaining to domestic usage in the United States went virtually unnoticed. The Ebonics movement took place exclusively among African Americans; white scholars were not part of the enterprise. Four years after Williams (1975) published *Ebonics: The True Language of Black Folks*, the *Journal of Black Studies* (Tolliver-Weddington 1979) devoted an entire issue to Ebonics. Asante (1979:363) observed:

> [I]nformation about Black English has proliferated, creating a misunderstanding of the scope and function of the language. Ebonics as a designation for the language, *usually referred to as Black English*, attempts to remove some of the ambiguity created by connecting black with English. [emphasis added]

Far from removing ambiguity, this portrait of Ebonics convolutes the international foundations Williams originally defined. Readers who are interested in a thorough history of Ebonics would be well advised to consult Tolliver-Weddington's (1979) edition; it brings together educators and specialists in communication disorders who address combinations of issues that grow directly from the linguistic legacy of American slavery, but it also accentuates the definitional derailment of Ebonics from an international entity to one that Tolliver-Weddington describes as follows:

> a language (dialect) that is spoken by Black Americans living in low-income communities and that [has] some specific characteristics observed in the phonological and grammatical system. Such agreement has led to numerous false assumptions and misunderstandings about Ebonics. (1979:364)

There are, to the best of my knowledge, four divergent definitions of Ebonics that exist among Afrocentric proponents of the term:

1. Ebonics is an international construct, including the linguistic consequences of the African slave trade (Williams 1975, 1997a).
2. Ebonics is the equivalent of black English and is considered to be a dialect of English (Tolliver-Weddington 1979).
3. Ebonics is the antonym of black English and is considered to be a language other than English (Smith 1992, 1997).

4. Ebonics refers to language among all people of African descent throughout the African Diaspora (Blackshire-Belay 1996).

The Oakland school board members adopted the third definition in their first Ebonics resolution but then retreated to the second position in their revised resolution—before deciding ultimately to abandon Ebonics. Despite the Oakland educators' efforts to distance themselves from the linguistic controversy they brought to world attention, the vast majority of the important practical issues pertaining to African American language remain unresolved. When Williams described his motivation and rationale for creating the BITCH, he was far more concerned about test bias than he was about Ebonics: "The BITCH is a culturally-specific test. It is not intended to be culturally-fair or [*sic*] a culturally common test. . . . For the BITCH, the content of all items was drawn exclusively from the Black Experience Domain" (Williams 1975:123).

Ironically, his chapter doesn't even mention Ebonics; rather, the language attributed to the BITCH is, specifically, associated with "some words, terms and expressions taken from the Black experience" (Williams 1975:124). Although ensuing versions of the BITCH came to be linked strongly with Ebonics, because Williams invented the BITCH test and subsequently coined Ebonics, his main focus concentrated on racial bias in standardized tests, and especially test bias against black students.

Scholars who study communication disorders were among the first to connect racial bias in testing to Ebonics, albeit from a clinical perspective. Seymour and Seymour state, "Ebonics is a variety of English spoken by a majority of Black Americans" (1979b:397). This definition fits with that espoused by Secretary Riley, as well as that endorsed by the LSA (see appendix A). In that same edition, Seymour and Seymour (1979a) wrote "Ebonics and P.L. 94–142," which is the public law that had come to be known as the Education of the Handicapped Act (EHA).

Since then that law has been reformed and is now known as the Individuals with Disabilities Educational Act (IDEA), and the revision of the act has profound implications for African American students who, in addition to speaking nonstandard English, may also suffer from other linguistic disabilities. What then of the normally developing black child who first learns vernacular African American English; is that child "handicapped"? Some might argue that African American English is indeed an educational handicap (for students), or a professional handicap (for adults), but it is another matter altogether to suggest that typical speakers of African American English suffer from a linguistic disability.

At present, officials with the National Institutes of Health (NIH) are seeking to develop new standardized tests for African American and Latino children who are not native standard English speakers. For far too long normally developing minority students have been relegated to special education in highly disproportionate numbers because they have been diagnosed as having linguistic disabilities when, in reality, the nationally normed diagnostics that speech pathologists employ make inadequate provision for children from other than standard English backgrounds. Some efforts have been made to salvage the existing diagnostics, say, by adjusting the scores for minority children, but such procedures are a far cry from the kinds of new diagnostics NIH hopes to create.

Regrettably, some of the most influential research in this field is linguistically unsophisticated and occasionally substitutes new linguistic errors for old ones. For example, Washington and Craig (1994) have conducted a series of tests on African American children to study their language development, and they identify and define several linguistic characteristics along with examples. One such case is that of "zero-ing: present progressive morpheme-ing is deleted," and the corresponding datum provided to illustrate "zero-ing" is "and the lady is sleep." This example has much less to do with the language development of black children and more to do with some of the special semantic and grammatical properties of the verb "sleep."

Consider, for example, the standard English equivalent of the preceding phrase. Two renditions can occur: (1) "and the lady is sleeping," or (2) "and the lady is asleep." Based on what we know about standard English, as well as nonstandard African American English, we would not expect to find zero-ing in truly progressive verbs. For example, it is unlikely that a child who speaks African American English would say, "and the lady is run" (for "and the lady is running"), or "and the lady is come" (for "and the lady is coming") in a manner similar to "the lady is sleep." The true explanation lies within semantic distinctions that have nothing to do with child language development.

"Sleep" and "wake" are special cases among English verbs are concerned, because they are semantically ambiguous with respect to their status as progressive or stative verbs; "and the lady is sleeping" suggests that "sleeping" is a progressive activity, but "and the lady is asleep" suggests that to be "asleep" is a stative act. Appalachian English might yield another nonstandard rendition, namely, "and the lady is a-sleeping."

Not to belabor the point, but this example has, if anything, less to do with "zero-ing" and far more to do with the fact that "asleep" or "sleeping" can be substituted freely in standard English renditions of the exemplary sentence. Again, this is due to the fact that "sleeping" is ambiguous with respect to its status as a progressive or stative verb. To attribute zero-ing to such a phrase is misleading and would diminish the value of pathological diagnostics derived from such a linguistic interpretation.

If we focus, instead, on the use of "is" versus "be" in the preceding example, the child who said, "and the lady is sleep" is closer to standard English than might be expected. Many black children would routinely say, "and the lady be sleep." The latter example is far more common among speakers of vernacular African American English. Also, because "be" is not always synonymous with "is" among African Americans, issues surrounding the usage—or lack of usage—of "be" or "is" have more to do with linguistic development than does so-called zero-ing.

The glass is half full regarding studies of communication disorders among African American children. Some scholars are keenly aware of limitations and racial bias in clinical speech testing instruments, but they do not yet have adequate tests to meet the needs of linguistically diverse children. Unfortunately, in the absence of greater linguistic sophistication, this trend may continue. As long as the nonstandard English of African American children is mislabeled and misunderstood, it will continue to be misdiagnosed.

Beyond limitations found in some of the developmental language studies of black children lies another problem, resulting from inadequate professional training. Speech clinicians are typically trained as generalists; they tend to know little of fundamental linguistics or relevant historical linguistic changes that have produced the myriad American dialects. Many speech clinicians and pathologists are not adequately trained to evaluate minority children or children with strong regional accents. This inadequate training results in a disturbing trend of pathological and educational misdiagnoses that overidentify blacks and Latinos for special education and other forms of remediation.

It is heartening to know that NIH, beyond the glare of the Ebonics spotlight, has recognized the need for speech pathologists to learn more about the special linguistic characteristics of vernacular African American English and various Latino dialects, but inadequate testing instruments are just the tip of a larger diagnostic iceberg. I pray that NIH expenditures will not merely produce "an African American test" and "a Hispanic test" but will also offer specific suggestions to reform the training of speech clinicians and perhaps allow some clinicians to specialize in language disorders among minority children, or those with specific regional accents. Through the efforts of many scholars who study communication disorders, considerable progress has been made to improve clinical speech diagnoses among minority children.

Perhaps the largest national investment in this topic centers on education, because all the legal and psychological and linguistic issues that hinge on Ebonics take center stage in the educational arena. The black-versus-white language debates in education were parasitically attached to Jensen's (1969) racist assertions that whites are genetically superior to blacks based on IQ test scores. Labov (1969) destroyed that hypothesis, and anyone who has been convinced by Hernstein and Murray's (1994) warmed over rendition of Jensen's work in *The Bell Curve* would do well to read Labov's classical study, "The Logic of Nonstandard English." There Labov debunked the deficit cognitive hypotheses through a rigorous analysis of the logical content in the speech of a socially stratified sample of African American speakers. His analyses have withstood the test of time, and they offer an empirical counterbalance to the deficit cognitive hypothesis that has plagued generations of black students.

Basil Bernstein (1970) put forward a hypothesis that members of the British upper class acquired an "elaborated code," whereas children from Britain's lower social classes acquired a "restricted code." Whereas some linguists have found these concepts to be extremely useful for comparative purposes, there have been some false cognitive assertions that grew from Bernstein's research that immediately took on racial overtones during controversial experiments by educational psychologists who falsely concluded that many African American students arrived at school lacking any sense of a coherent language (Bereiter and Engleman 1966).

Explicitly, the strong cognitive interpretation of Bernstein's work implies that upper-class speakers of the elaborated code have a greater capacity for abstract thought than do working- and lower-class speakers of the restricted code. These theories tend to be more controversial in the United States, where a national ethos of equality seems to contradict such cognitive beliefs. Also, within the United States there are so many regional variations in the dialects spoken by members of various provincial upper classes because we Americans don't trace our local standard dialects back to the royal linguistic lineage as do most Europeans. It should therefore come as no surprise that Bernstein's studies have been more influential in Europe more so than in the postcolonial linguistic context of the United States, a society that has grown by absorbing speakers from every conceivable linguistic background.

As previously mentioned, however, in the United States, Bernstein's class distinctions for language came to take on racial and cognitive overtones that are antithetical to the pervasive American creed that we are all created equal and should have equal opportunities to pursue life's opportunities to the fullest of our abilities. This "rugged individualist" stereotype, which has become a cliché, helps to account for the cool reception that Bernstein's work receives among scholars and educators who seek to defy the class and language boundaries that thrive in every advanced industrialized society.

Another educational paradox grows from a parallel ethos that every American child is guaranteed a (good?) public education as a birthright. The stark reality is that educational Darwinism prevails; those with the financial means to invest in a high-quality education for their children pay considerable sums, above and beyond their tax contributions to public education, in the form of individualized affirmative action for their children (in the form of private tutors or private schools). This economically based educational abyss is also reflected in public schools, with affluent communities routinely offering educational benefits unavailable to schools in which financial or educational resources are inadequate (Baugh 1999).

The United States is one of the only major industrialized nations that does not have a central ministry of education. During a series of lectures I gave in Europe, I encountered a cynical interpretation of American public education among some members of the intelligentsia. For example, distinguished economists pondered the American "pretense" of offering equal educational opportunities to all when it was patently obvious to them that the American economy cannot support a society in which the majority of citizens are well educated and consequently well paid through lucrative careers. They interpreted America's decentralized system of education in Marxist terms—as an inherently biased enterprise that is duplicitous at its core. The rich, however mediocre, will get richer through overt control over educational resources; the poor—however talented—will continue to get poorer without greater access to competitive educational opportunities.

Although I have long been critical of the detrimental effects of racial bias in education, growing from the legacy of American apartheid and entrenched practices that perpetuate this bias, I found myself in the curious position of defending American education while I was abroad. In much the same manner that I feel free to occasionally criticize my own children, I take considerable umbrage if others do so, either overtly or covertly. An analogous reaction prevailed as I listened to European scholars criticize the American educational system. My hypocrisy is thus exposed, for while I feel free to offer educational criticism—wrapped in the warmth of my First Amendment rights—I admit that I became angry as I listened to foreign colleagues belittle our efforts to improve race relations and eliminate detrimental forms of racial bias.

Although no rational person would defend the weak links in the American educational chain, our decentralized system of education has in fact produced some of the finest public and private schools anywhere. Our system of higher education remains the envy of the world: Public and private institutions of considerable stature and quality continue to attract students from foreign nations. No, I am not now defending the educational status quo; rather, I endorse the potential pedagogical innovation and creativity that can be found in various schools, typically those not constrained by excessive external regulations that inhibit teacher's abilities to be successful. However, as long as some teachers continue to believe that nonstandard English, or LEP, is a sign of diminished cognitive potential, the future welfare of this nation is threatened—not by the more visible forms of racial intolerance that occupy the attention of presidential commissions, but by less visible forms of linguistic intolerance for others who speak in ways that some find unappealing, or worse.

The Ebonics controversy brings these linguistic issues into direct racial alignment with American slave descendants, but the preceding observations about linguistic intolerance of nonstandard English, or LEP exceed the boundaries of the black population and extend to anyone who speaks with a dialect that may be stigmatized. And it is here that a theory of sociolinguistic relativity comes into play (see chapter 3), because a regional dialect that may be appealing—and even cherished—in one part of the country can often become the object of linguistic derision and ridicule in other parts of the Republic.

Few educational curricula attempt to teach greater linguistic tolerance in harmony with increased racial tolerance. I believe the Ebonics episode did little—at least initially—to enhance racial tolerance or greater linguistic acceptance of African Americans by nonblacks. However, speaking now as a black man who has lived in different regions of this country, I recognize that many Americans—in their personal quest to overcome this nation's racist history—seek to treat everyone (including African Americans) as equals. It is partially for this reason that affirmative action is so often vilified, because of growing public hostility toward any form of racial preferences, especially when affirmative action amplifies perceptions of reverse discrimination against whites.

One relevant linguistic barrier, reflected by another dimension of the theory of sociolinguistic relativity, lies in the existence of competing linguistic loyalties. Fordham and Ogbu (1986) observed that many minority students resisted educational efforts to advance their standard English proficiency because they did not want to "sound white." They observed that many minority students maintain a strong sense of linguistic loyalty to their vernacular culture, and through this effort not only do they preserve and advance their local or ethnic dialect, but they do so in open linguistic defiance of authority. And it is "defiance of authority" that results in disproportionately high numbers of minority students being suspended from schools and resulting in higher dropout rates. Regrettably, statistics confirm that dropouts are also far more likely than their peers who stay in school to join the growing ranks of incarcerated Americans.

Is it possible to change these trends and offer hope to students who have not learned standard English? Ever the optimist, I think we can; indeed, I think we must. To accomplish this worthy goal we need a combination of educational and political leadership that can support local educators who demonstrate the ability to help all students learn. This educational ambition grows from a "lift all boats" philosophy in contrast to the rich-versus-poor class debates that have thrived under *Liberal Racism* (Sleeper 1997).

It has been my experience that fights between the rich and poor are almost always won by the rich; they have the resources, time, and attorneys to make the system work for them. The poor have never been able to take full advantage of their rights—be they housing rights, voting rights, or educational rights, among others. It is against this backdrop of linguistic diversity, among socially stratified populations of Americans who speak with various regional accents, that we linguists began to tread.

By comparison with our sister social sciences, we linguists are relative newcomers, but under Chomsky's extraordinary influence we have obtained a singular reputation for intellectual flamboyance that straddles a precarious fence between truth and myth. I was first attracted to linguistics and its rigorous scientific basis by way of Labov's (1969) exceptional studies of the logical content of African American English. However, there is another dimension of linguistic theory that is less well understood among the public, but which helps to account for the LSA resolution affirming the existence and linguistic integrity of vernacular African American English (see appendix A). That is, from a theoretical linguistic point of view, all human languages and dialects are equal in the eyes of our science. Sociolinguists, such as myself, study language usage in various social contexts, and we routinely observe social circumstances that contradict our professional predilection toward inalienable linguistic equality.

Brief conversations with nonlinguists worldwide readily expose a mosaic of linguistic preferences and prejudices. Linguistic impressions— be they positive or negative—tend to govern changing patterns of language attitudes globally, and the United States, despite its history as a melting pot, has yet to fully eliminate lingering vestiges of regional, racial, and ethnic prejudice, which is partially embodied within the inventory of languages and dialects we tend to favor or disfavor.

It would be misleading, indeed, it would be false, to suggest that we linguists have always been among the linguistically enlightened— some of the earliest linguistic treatises expose the antiquity of professional linguistic elitism. Those familiar with Latin will recognize that "classical Latin" and "vulgar Latin" parallel class differences between literate and illiterate members of a socially stratified speech community. Some may speak an elaborated code in contrast to a restricted code, or—as we linguists prefer to describe the differences—some might speak with "standard dialects" while the poor continue to employ "nonstandard dialects."

Are "vulgar" dialects identical to "nonstandard dialects"? I think not; yet some of the oldest and most cherished linguistic tomes enshrine countless shibboleths in terms that clearly denigrate poor and socially disenfranchised speakers. Ironically, the poor tend to be the very people who are largely responsible for linguistic evolution and change (Labov 1994). For it was not until the publication of Johnson's original English dictionary, made accessible by the invention of the printing press, that we begin to see significant linguistic conservation in the face of more rapid changes in spoken English pronunciation. Were this not the case, words such as "knight," "climb," or "laugh" might be spelled differently (e.g., "nite," "clime," or "laf").

The next stage of professional linguistic enlightenment substituted extremely negative terms for mildly negative terms, and it became common to see scholarly references to "substandard dialects" in the linguistic literature. Eventually, in Bloomfield's (1933) *Language*, we find the introduction of the more neutral term, "nonstandard English," but now that term has come under fire by proponents of Ebonics and others who also reject such terms as "black English," or "African American English."

Elsewhere (Baugh 1991), I describe the evolution of respectful terms of self-reference that we African Americans have adopted through the years. When I was a child, during the 1950s, the term "Negro" was considered to be respectful, as was the term "colored." Now many black Americans take offense at "Negro" or "colored." These changes tended to take place within the racial isolation of the vernacular African American culture, and they remain a source of internal debate among American blacks who, like me, are extremely proud of our African ancestry. Other Americans, including some slave descendants, do not share this view; they project a misplaced sense of shame on those who were enslaved and, by extension, to their posterity. Such self-hating African Americans are rare, but they are often among the most visible public critics of fellow slave descendants.

Linguists have employed alternative terms to describe the speech of American slave descendants: Bloomfield (1933) spoke of "nonstandard English," and Labov (1966) was more explicit in his reference to

"Nonstandard Negro English" until Wolfram and Fasold (1969) first introduced the concept of "Black English" into linguistics and the world. "Black English" eventually was adopted as the title of Dillard's (1972) book, and in an effort to differentiate between the more formal speech spoken at home and the prevalence for the use of informal vernacular in public discourse, I adopted an ethnographically based title for *Black Street Speech* (Baugh 1983), because so many of the African Americans with whom I consulted made vital distinctions between "street language," "home language," and "school language." Based on these ethnographic influences, several African American linguists did not follow the Afrocentric trend toward Ebonics.

Based on linguistic developments within the African American community, some black linguists, myself included, began to use the term "African American" long before Jesse Jackson made headlines when he called for its formal adoption in favor of "Black American" (see Baugh 1991, Smitherman 1991). In the case of Ebonics, however, we find a term that is not linked ethnographically to terminology that evolved organically from within the larger African American population.

The most objectionable term, of course, is "nigger"—a term so offensive that we have all witnessed its euphemistic transformation during the O. J. Simpson trial to "the N . . . word" (see Gibbs 1996). Just as Ebonics applies only to people of African descent, so too does the "N . . . word," but most writers have been careful to disassociate the "N . . . word" from "Ebonics." Among Americans, the legacy of slavery is unique to those of us who have African ancestry, in part due to the obvious visible racial attributes that made slaves stand out among free citizens. The branding of white indentured servants was intended to make them stand out as well, but branding or tattoos might often be concealed in ways that black skin could not. Only slave descendants have ever suffered the indignities of the derogatory racial slur "nigger."

Although black people agree on several terms they find offensive, or extremely offensive, their efforts to adopt positive terms have often been contentious, both within and beyond America's black communities. Ebonics was initially coined with these positive attributes in mind with the intention of creating a positive term. The linguistic history of slavery denied blacks direct access to their ancestral heritage, and proponents of Ebonics attempted to instill linguistic pride through their efforts. Again, we slave descendants, as involuntary immigrants, are the only immigrants who cannot trace our linguistic ancestry, especially with the same accuracy as more recent voluntary immigrants.

Although black scholars introduced the term "Ebonics" with worthy social intentions, they did so by violating one of the most essential principles known to linguistic science. I describe this issue more thoroughly in "Language and Race: Some Implications for Linguistic Science" (Baugh 1988). There I suggest that one should never define a language or speech community based solely on the racial classification of its speakers. The history of colonialism proves this fact. The global spread of English, French, Russian, Portuguese, and Spanish—to name a few languages diffused by colonialism—confirms that speech communities and racial communities are not coincident. The fundamental premise of Afrocentric scholarship, which focuses exclusively on people with complete or partial African ancestry, flies in the face of the fundamental linguistic principle that a language never be equated with a single racial group.

Because most linguists first heard of Ebonics by way of Oakland's efforts (see chapters 2 and 3), they simply assumed that it was identical to "Black English"; most linguists (and the public) were simply unaware of the diverse theoretical history of this term. On reflection, however, it would have been far more helpful to educators and the public had we linguists not equivocated on the vital distinction between "a language" and "a dialect" (see appendix A). Black English has long been considered an English dialect, and comments regarding linguistic classifications in China, Norway, and Sweden (see appendix A) did little to help resolve the dismal educational prospects that most black children still face.

Thus far, we have reviewed the evolution and interrelationship between alternative theories regarding Afrocentric classifications of African American language, including differences in the theoretical formulation of standardized clinical tests for African American children. We have also considered the relevance of corresponding educational debates regarding linguistic-cognitive differences versus linguistic-cognitive deficits in connection with poor academic performance among low-income and minority students.

The best available evidence supports the importance of nurturing— by family, school, and community—over any presumption of genetically inherited cognitive advantages that one might attribute to race. The more accurate statement about the discrepancy is that it thrives through perpetuation of an inequitable educational system with entrenched class bias favoring the wealthy. As an African American scholar who has both attended and taught at several prestigious institutions of higher learning, I am painfully aware of the blatant contradictions and stereotypes that have been perpetuated by antiquated affirmative action remedies that satisfy no one.

This is not to imply that we no longer need to devise new remedies that can ensure greater opportunities for those who in the past have been disenfranchised from influential positions of wealth, power, and political influence. Rather, efforts to overcome past discrimination must be re-formed to ensure that help for some does not come at the expense of detrimental consequences for others. Toward this end I would encourage those who seek to unilaterally dismantle affirmative action programs to take an equally hard look at entrenched nepotism.

When viewed within the broader social context of efforts to eliminate racial bias in education, Ebonics suffers from several definitional detriments that can no longer be dismissed by mere hand waving. I therefore hope that these remarks expose some of the scholarly and educational perils of attempting to adopt Ebonics as either a technical linguistic term or as an educational philosophy, at least as long as multiple and contradictory definitions for Ebonics continue to exist. Just as a house that is divided cannot stand, linguistic terminology that alleges to have scientific validity cannot survive with multiple definitions.

Racist Reactions and Ebonics Satire

This chapter explores a series of racist-to-benign reactions sparked by Ebonics. As a linguist devoted to the educational welfare of the poor, I typically reject most ignorant comments that confirm racist linguistic stereotypes. However, any Ebonics survey would be incomplete without describing some of the vicious as well as innocent cases of Ebonics insults that sprang forth after Oakland's ill-fated resolutions captured public attention. Racist web sites appeared with alarming speed as Ebonics became an open target of public ridicule. Some Oakland educators were claiming to have elevated public awareness of this issue to new heights, but the following examples show that African American language had been maligned and dragged down to new depths through the promulgation of various unsavory opinions.

One of the earliest racist ventures to come to light was The Ebonics Translator, a service by which anyone could send electronic mail containing a standard English text to a main translation center and within twenty-four hours receive an Ebonics translation by return e-mail. The Ebonics Translator provided the following rendition of the Lord's Prayer, which some may find offensive:

The Lord's Prayer in English and Ebonics

English	Ebonics
The Lord's Prayer	*Bid Daddy's Rap*
Our Father, who art in heaven	Yo, Bid Daddy upstairs,
Hallowed be thy name	You be chillin'
Thy Kingdom come	So be yo hood
Thy will be done	You be sayin' it, I be doin' it
On earth as it is in heaven and	In dis 'ere hood yo's
Give us this day our daily bread	Gimme some eats
And forgive us our trespasses	And cut me some slack, Blood
As we forgive those who trespass against us	Sos I be doin' it dem dat trespass against us
And lead us not into temptation	don't be pushing me into no jive
But deliver us from evil	and keep dem Crips away
For thine is the Kingdom, the power and the glory, forever and ever,	'Cause you always be da Man
Amen.	Das right.

In the name of humor, this so-called translation offends blacks and Christians simultaneously. Does "deliver us from evil" mean "keep them Crips away"? Or, do African Americans say "Das Right" instead of "Amen," especially after a prayer? I don't think so. Those of us who have spent considerable time in African American churches will attest that "Amen" is alive and well among black people.

Other racist reactions to Ebonics fell into two broad categories: (1) mean-spirited, overtly racist attacks that were akin to any of the worst racist discourse ever produced in American history and (2) benign linguistic prejudice toward vernacular African American English, based on combinations of false linguistic stereotypes. Critics within the latter category typically offered anti-Ebonics educational alternatives, each extolling the virtues of standard English. Rarely did criticism of Ebonics acknowledge Oakland's assertions that increased standard English proficiency was, in fact, the primary educational goal.

Some of the most insidious examples of racist commentaries were found within general news publications that drew pathological analogies to Ebonics. The *Economist* produced an article titled "The Ebonics Virus" (1997) and the pathological analogy was maintained in an editorial cartoon comparing the Bubonic plague to "The Ebonic Plague" (see figure 4).

Beyond implications that Ebonics represents a lethal threat to (standard?) English is the suggestion that Ebonics is a primitive linguistic throwback to some bygone era when English (spoken by African Americans?) was much less refined than it is today (see figure 5). The cartoonist conveys his obvious contempt for Ebonics through unilateral depiction of a one-way retrograde throttle; the Ebonics time machine is only capable of transporting its passengers back through time.

Newsweek and *Mad Magazine* had the curious fate of producing Ebonics articles with identical titles—"Hooked on Ebonics." The *Newsweek* article (Leland and Joseph 1997) provided content from interviews with Oakland's educational officials, but *Mad Magazine*'s article presented a parodic rendition of "Hooked on Phonics℠," which promised prospective customers that the introduction of Ebonics into schools would provide a welcome transformation from dull, lifeless classrooms (which were depicted as being filled with students who were comatose testaments to perpetual boredom) into lively, thriving, learning communities composed of highly attentive students and energetic (hip) teachers.

A freckle-faced white student is portrayed as the hero in this farce, and he begins by presenting a stodgy academic report:

> George Washington became our first President in 1789. He was chosen because of the leadership he showed as General during the Revolutionary War. Following America's victory, Washington was instrumental in lobbying for ratification of the Constitution. Resourceful and brave, his personal discipline was essential to the new Union. We can all be grateful that he was there for our nation's growing pains.

Figure 4. *Cartoon from* The Landmark, *Holden, Massachusetts. January 2, 1997. Reprinted by permission.*

But, after its Ebonics face-lift, that same report comes alive, as do the classmates who were snoozing through the traditional standard English presentation:

> George was da head G, you know what I' sayin' Da head chump in Englan' be frontin', so Wash goes, "uh-uh, homey, I got mad skillz!" So da King goes, "You ain't be grabbin' my hood, timbertooth!" So Wash goes, "You know where I be, Poindexter!" So da King sendz his boyz over for a sail-by, but BOOM! Wash wastes their sorry ass. In conclusion, Georgie was da BOMB!

I, for one, was somewhat surprised to see that Devlin's (1997) *Mad Magazine* contribution portrayed many of the relevant linguistic facts more accurately than most of the more formal Ebonics critiques. Indeed, some of the most pathetic attempts at Ebonics humor were those that feigned intellectual superiority while pandering to misplaced linguistic elitism. One unfortunate but highly visible example of this trend ap-

Non Sequitur

Figure 5. Non Sequitur *cartoon by Robb Armstrong, April 1, 1997.* © *Washington Post Writers Group. Reprinted by permission.*

peared in the *New Republic* (1997). The author, Jakob Heilbrunn, badly misrepresented, diminished, and eventually dismissed the massive available linguistic evidence in sweeping overgeneralizations that distorted significant research by anthropologists, applied linguists, creolists, dialectologists, educators, formal linguists, and sociolinguists under a single demeaning banner, dubbing them "Ebonologists."

Several linguists from various theoretical backgrounds have so thoroughly trashed Heilbrunn that it's difficult to top their efforts (see Nunberg 1997). Heilbrunn's reactionary genuflection could have been predicted, especially as Oakland provided such a tantalizing target for race pundits of every political persuasion. Nevertheless, Heilbrunn went beyond the bounds of tasteful satire in tribute to an ideological calling. His vilification of Ebonics was excessive and ultimately boiled down to another mendacious exercise in racial agitation.

Bill Cosby (1997) also weighed in on the Ebonics debate, offering the following tongue-in-cheek remarks, which were published under the title "Elements of Igno-Ebonics Style":

> I remember one day 15 years ago, a friend of mine told me a racist joke.
>
> > Question: Do you know what Toys "R" Us is called in Harlem?
> > Answer: We Be Toys.
>
> So, before the city of Oakland, Calif., starts to teach its teachers Ebonics, or what I call "Igno-Ebonics," I think the school board should study all the ramifications of endorsing an urbanized version of the English language.

> After all, Ebonics be a complex issue.
>
> If teachers are going to legitimize Ebonics, then all authority fig-
> ures who interact with children—such as law-enforcement officers—
> will have to learn it as well. In fact, the consequences of a grammatical
> accident could be disastrous during a roadside encounter with a po-
> liceman.
>
> The first thing people ask when they are pulled over is, "Why did
> you stop me, officer?" Imagine an Ebonics-speaking Oakland teenager
> being stopped on the freeway by a non-Ebonics-speaking California
> Highway Patrol officer. The teenager, posing that same question Ebon-
> ically, would begin by saying: "Lemme ax you . . ." The patrolman,
> fearing he is about to be hacked to death, could charge the kid with
> threatening a police officer. Thus, to avoid misunderstanding, notices
> would have to be added to driver's licenses warning: "This driver
> speaks Ebonics only." (*Wall Street Journal*, p. A10)

His article continues with other references to new jobs for "Ebonics
specialists" and the more serious educational admonition that "legiti-
mizing the street in the classroom is backwards. We should be working
hard to legitimize the classroom—and English—in the street." Inner-
city educators are keenly aware that such a linguistic transformation is
both daunting and still relatively rare for the vast majority of African
American students.

Cosby's initial focus on the potentially fatal ambiguity associated
with the pronunciation of "ask" as "ax" (i.e, "aks") is among the most
frequently cited characteristics of African American English. "Aks"
is often alleged to be a major source of linguistic confusion between
blacks and whites or, specifically, between those who speak standard
English and those who speak nonstandard vernacular African American
English.

Oprah Winfrey discussed this very linguistic example with a white
woman in her audience during a show on black English. The white
woman confessed that she simply could not comprehend black speech,
and she mentioned "aks" in particular:

> Audience member: I do not always understand what's being said. In
> fact, I'm in the communications field. I do a lot of work by phone,
> and sometimes when I reach a black person on the other end I have

to say two or three times, "Excuse me, excuse me."* I don't want to insult them, but I really don't understand what they're saying.

Oprah: Why is it? Because they are using a different language, or is it the dialect, or is it the use of grammar, or what?

Audience member: Um . . . They do say . . . They say things like "aks" instead of "ask."

Without going into too much detail, the pronunciation of "aks" for "ask" is the result of metathesis, which is a form of phonological inversion, that is, similar to the way that many young children say "pasghetti" rather than "spaghetti." As children grow older, gaining greater motor control and more metalinguistic awareness, we can more effectively teach them the appropriate standard norms. Eventually they begin to say "spaghetti" properly. In the case of "aks" among many African Americans, however, there was never sufficient early exposure to literacy to correct this mistake. Because slaves were denied access to the schools, in which most other Americans learned standard English, the "ask" to "aks" transformation was nullified due to a lack of "corrective" exposure to standard English. This trend began to change as more blacks gained access to better educational opportunities along with increased interaction with standard American English.

Grammatical considerations also account for the "ask" versus "ax" confusion; "ax" is a noun† and "ask" is a verb. A grammatical difference of this kind is not trivial in this instance; in fact, such a difference provides the necessary window of linguistic opportunity that allowed metathesis to occur in the first place—that is, because nouns and verbs are not transmutable (or rarely so in puns), their different grammatical functions disambiguate intended meanings. Thus, if an African American said, "Let me aks you a question," I would worry much more about the person who, upon hearing this utterance, concludes that the speaker actually intended to say "ax" than I would about the black person who

---

*During the O. J. Simpson trial the issue of racial identification based on speech was a major concern—so much so that Simpson's attorneys implied that anyone willing to draw racial inference based exclusively on hearing someone's voice would be racist. However, Oprah's guest had no such reservation, claiming to know when she had reached a "black person on the other end."

†"Ax" is also used idiomatically referring to abrupt termination of employment: "He was axed," or "He got the ax."

displayed nonstandard metathesis. Nevertheless, it is partially because of racial stereotypes reinforced by the linguistic stigma associated with "ask" versus "aks" that it still remains one of the strongest markers of class and educational distinction among African Americans—that is, effectively differentiating those who have had the benefits of a superior education from those who have had less educational exposure.

Does this mean that Bill Cosby and Oprah's guest were "wrong" about "aks?" Well, yes and no: Yes, because it is misleading to attribute too much miscommunicative potential to "aks," simply because it never occurs in linguistic domains where it is truly ambiguous with "ax." No, in the sense that they are correct to call attention to stigmatized differences between African American English and standard English.

"Ax me no questions . . ." and "Please sharpen the ask" simply don't occur naturally in English for good reason. They're ungrammatical and therefore meaningless. Rather, "aks," like "pasghetti," stands out to those for whom it is either rare or nonexistent, and it often goes unnoticed among those who find no compelling linguistic reason to distinguish the noun "ax" from an identical pronunciation of the verb "ask" when pronounced as "aks."

It didn't take long before other comedians began to generate a series of satirical Ebonic spin-offs for other groups: Jews were said to speak "Hebonics," and Italians were said to speak "Italionics," while residents of Utah were said to speak "Utahonics," and gay men were alleged to speak "Shebonics," among numerous others. But the shortest suffix derived from Ebonics that I encountered was limited to the final syllable "-ics" in a Bruce Tinsley comic strip, depicting a fellow professional educator with linguistic expertise (see figure 6).

In the preceding example, "profane" language—and not race—is being castigated, and presumably "Ebonics" is the alleged source of that profanity. Although the preceding satirical depiction of "Profanics" in this strip makes no overt racial reference, its Ebon"-ics" derivation has inherent racial connotations; the comic strip attempts to mask this reality. The implication, of course, is that the portrayed educator, who is not African American, is addressing a matter of language that is not constrained by race.

Much of the frustration, tension, and volatility that Ebonics—and its choice of genetic terminology—evoked, was aptly portrayed in a Doonesbury comic strip (see figure 7).

Mallard Fillmore   **By Bruce Tinsley**

Figure 6. Mallard Fillmore *strip by Bruce Tinsley, February 7, 1997.* © *King Features Syndicate Inc. Reprinted by permission.*

Unlike some of the hateful satire that Ebonics spawned, Trudeau captures some of the exasperation that many Americans felt when they first encountered Ebonics through Oakland's educational maneuvering. Many Americans from different racial backgrounds were simply trying to comprehend Oakland's linguistic reasoning, and Trudeau conveys this sentiment at the same time that he pokes fun at the extreme Afrocentric interpretations of Ebonics that were inherent in Oakland's resolutions. His reference to "Ancient Egyptian Idiom" also hints at the central linguistic issue that triggered this controversy in the first place. Is Ebonics English, or not?

This particular comic strip had ironic significance for me because I was called on by numerous educators, politicians, and journalists, all of whom were caught off guard by Oakland's assertions. I have never wavered on this point: American slave descendants speak English and not a distinctive African language. However, vernacular African American English has incontrovertible African influences. It was due, in part, to these African influences and to public confusion over the differences between dialects and languages that in 1997 the LSA balked at this very point:

> The distinction between "languages" and "dialects" is usually made more on social and political grounds than on purely linguistic ones. For example, different varieties of Chinese are popularly regarded as "dialects," though their speakers cannot understand each other,

Figure 7. Doonesbury *strip by G. B. Trudeau, February 16, 1997* © *Universal Press Syndicate. Reprinted by permission.*

but speakers of Swedish and Norwegian, which are regarded as separate "languages," generally understand each other." (See appendix A.)

Many black and white Americans generally understand each other too, and my colleagues would have done well to emphasize the importance of intelligibility regarding linguistic classifications. I completely concur with Taylor and Labov's independent Senate testimony, affirming that African Americans speak English, albeit reflecting the lingering linguistic consequences of American slavery. As Labov noted during his Senate testimony (1977; see chapter 5), linguists who study the speech of American slave descendants had not previously adopted Ebonic terminology. In retrospect it is evident that most people were clueless about the original international definition of Ebonics, thereby making it much more difficult to separate accurate linguistic facts from distorted Ebonic fiction. Perhaps the greatest linguistic myth, shared by many blacks and nonblacks, is the belief that nonstandard African American English is just "wrong" or "bad English." Consider, for example, the following table of opposing linguistic attributes:

Table 1. *Positive and Negative Linguistic Labels for Speech*

Positive Linguistic Terms	Negative Linguistic Terms
standard	nonstandard
grammatical	ungrammatical
formal	informal
proper	improper
acceptable	unacceptable
careful	casual
good	bad
correct	incorrect
right	wrong
smart	stupid
superior	inferior
best	worst
and so on . . .	

Linguistic historians have demonstrated that the evolution of linguistic standards is best understood in political terms, because those standards are determined by political circumstances that have nothing whatsoever to do with the inherent linguistic norms of a given language. Those who control political power also influence the standards by which languages are judged, supported, and advanced within educational academies.

When the social stratification of languages, and dialects within those languages, is objectively viewed in terms of their political and economic parentage, it becomes impossible to fairly allocate linguistic attributions by means of most of the highly subjective terms (see table 1) that are commonly misused for this purpose, not only in America but in every society in which linguistic differences are also a reflection of real—or potential—social strife. We linguists often feel like marginalized social scientists when it comes to such weighty matters, which may explain Chomsky's dual career in linguistics and political science.

I too have chosen a multifaceted career, with prongs in anthropology, applied linguistics, education, and related policy studies. Because

Wayne Stayskal / Tampa Tribune

Figure 8. Cartoon by Wayne Stayskal/Tampa Tribune, February 9, 1997.
© *Tampa Tribune. Reprinted by permission.*

of these interdisciplinary professional affiliations, I was especially in-
trigued by the multifarious subliminal messages that are conveyed in an
editorial cartoon from the *Tampa Tribune.* In this instance "mathematics" has been combined with "Ebonics," creating a new term: "mathabonics" (see figure 8).

My first reaction was linguistic; why "mathabonics" rather than
"mathebonics"? My son, who was nine-years old at the time, felt the
latter example offered too much phonological latitude, because some
say "Ebonics" with a long /⟨e⟩/ (as in 'eat'), while others employ a short
/⟩e⟨/ (as in 'educate').* However, by using "a" rather than "e," the artist

---

*The initial vowel of "Ebonics" has also been observed with an initial /ə/ or
short /i/ as in "it."

effectively constrains the range of possible pronunciations, that is, according to my son's hypothesis. It's also possible that "mathebonics" might convey a stronger racial connotation than "mathabonics," because the former entirely includes "-ebonics," whereas "mathabonics" employs a reduced "-bonics" suffix that could, arguably, carry less overt racial baggage.

As observed with several other editorial Ebonics cartoons and comics, the characters portrayed above are all white. I assume that the cartoonist was attempting to avoid any accusation of racist intent, but the lack of any reference to blacks—when every available Ebonics definition applies exclusively to blacks—merely conceals the race card; it certainly doesn't eliminate it. Had he portrayed the student engaged in mathabonics as the only African American in the class he would have surely been accused of overt racism, but such a portrait would more accurately reflect social reality.

Another message that is conveyed, quite pointedly, is that "mathabonics" is wrong. By claiming that $(7 \times 3 = 16)$, the student demonstrates an overt error, but had the problem been written as $(7 \times 3 = \sqrt{441})$ the answer would not be wrong but it would be nonstandard. In my opinion there is a world of difference between a wrong answer and a nonstandard representation of an alternative answer. Through racial obfuscation, much of Ebonics satire has turned back the clock regarding prospects for greater linguistic tolerance or a better understanding of the dismal educational plight of so many African American students.

These issues go far beyond the realm of Ebonics satire, talk shows, or anti-Ebonics legislation. They point, specifically, to the future of American race relations. It's painfully clear that, in the name of satire, some remain willing, if not eager, to heap salt on tender social wounds that continue to be aggravated by racially motivated church burnings, police brutality, and heinous murders that serve as recent reminders that African Americans, Jews and other minorities, may still fall victim to racist attacks.

Beyond Ebonics
Striving toward Enhanced Linguistic Tolerance

Although my parents did their best to teach me the difference between proper and improper English, they never did so in terms of "black English versus white English" or "broken English versus correct English." Such racial or judgmental classifications were nevertheless common among my peers, regardless of racial background. Those early childhood experiences run counter to my professional predilection toward linguistic equality among the world's languages and dialects. Humanity has often defied theoretical idealism, and scholars from various backgrounds have repeatedly demonstrated that social divisions come to be reorganized, reinvented, and maintained through a host of interrelated criteria.

The linguistic window into this world of human diversity is inherently limited, yet it is intricately woven into the ecological fabric of day-to-day life in every society. Detailed studies of linguistic diversity within the United States paint a slightly different picture of African American English than do those that myopically portray it through restrictive ideological lenses. As mentioned throughout this book, competing definitions and hypotheses about Ebonics defy scientific credibility and consequently dilute their intended educational utility; moreover, this will continue to be the case until the time an empirically defensible Ebonics definition is fully articulated. To the best of my knowledge this formidable task remains undone. These definitional problems are considerable, and it would be misleading to suggest that most of the linguistic misconceptions about black people lie at the feet of the Afrocentric proponents who nurtured Ebonics.

Conservative African American pundits have also been guilty of spreading false Ebonics rumors, and some of the most disturbing race baiting has come at the hands of black scholars and journalists who have made several misleading Ebonics statements. Some blacks (and perhaps others), composed largely of political centrists, have witnessed vitriolic linguistic reactions from extremists at both ends of the political spectrum. But to dissect the linguistic and racial strands of Ebonics, a brief thought experiment might help. For the purpose of this exercise we must imagine a different U.S. history, one that has no citizens of color.

Under this hypothetical scenario Columbus met no Native Americans on landing in the new world. Similarly, my slave ancestors would have never been taken captive in Africa, nor would the Chinese have been imported to build the railroads. Japanese Americans would never have been interned during World War II, and so on. This thought experiment poses the prospect of a nation composed entirely and exclusively of citizens with white European ancestry; no racial diversity of any noteworthy significance would exist in this imaginary "all white" America. Farm workers would be white, as would most unskilled laborers, and so too would the highest paid executives: Every American would be white. Would linguistic prejudice prevail in an all-white America? If the answer is yes, what form(s) would it take?

Prior evidence from others who have provided responses to this thought experiment confirms that most citizens believe that linguistic prejudice would prevail in an all-white America, and that class, sex, region, residence, education, occupation, and religion, among other factors, would reinforce dialectal differences among an all-white citizenry. To a considerable degree this is presently now the case: Whites who grew up in the Northeast tend to speak differently than do whites who grew up in the Southeast, and often they maintain linguistic loyalties to their group or region while castigating others from elsewhere.

Having personally conducted this thought experiment in every region of the country, it appears that all Americans are keenly aware of linguistic prejudice among us, including strong differences of linguistic opinion among people from similar racial backgrounds. In this respect the Ebonics debate—just among blacks—results in differences of linguistic opinion that resonate with other racial, ethnic, and regional groups that decry the existence of "bad English" (or the lack of English) among themselves. If linguistic prejudice could prevail in an all-white America, then how should we go about healing our existing linguistic wounds, which have somehow survived despite our multiracial heritage with its corresponding multilingual history?

My greatest motivation for writing this book is pinned on the hope of enhancing national linguistic reconciliation. The United States, of all countries, should be a nation in which every child is allowed to celebrate his or her linguistic and cultural heritage, and none should ever be made to bear false burdens of linguistic shame through historical circumstances that have always been beyond their capacity to control. Those of us who support renewed efforts to reunite America know that race baiting and finger pointing will not advance greater social harmony, nor will it eliminate the psychological scar tissue created by terrorist acts specifically targeting black people, fomented by social strife (see Wright 1990).

The linguistic dimension of this task, which usually escapes detection by pundits and politicians, tends to be reinforced by our different sociolinguistic points of view (see chapter 3). Political maneuvering cannot force citizens to be more accepting of others whose speech they devalue, or perhaps abhor. No laws can instill linguistic goodwill within each of us or our fellow citizens, especially as many linguistic stereotypes are so deeply entrenched that nothing short of massive reeducation will guide us all toward greater linguistic tolerance.

Part of this effort demands that we challenge and expose linguistic ignorance whenever possible, regardless of its source, and much of this enterprise is not limited to the plight of African Americans but is relevant to any group that has previously been the object of linguistic ridicule. White Southerners, for example, have often been depicted in films from the 1940s as routinely dim-witted, and these portrayals have usually been achieved through exaggerated speech and other visible traits. Television shows from the 1960s perpetuated these trends, continuing to falsely portray southern speech as an inferior form of American English.

The author Shelby Steele confirms this observation by his own admission:

> Changing planes in a Southern airport, the sound of a white Southern accent slips right past what I know about the New South and finds my memory of the old South. (p. 149) . . . I could condemn this woman, or at least be willing to condemn her and even her region, not because of her racial beliefs, which I didn't know, but because her accent had suddenly made her accountable to my voluminous and vivid memory of a racist South. (p. 150) . . . The white Southern accent I heard in the airport is an example of an objective correlative—an objective event that by association evokes a particular emotion or set of emotions. It was the savvy, musical sound of this woman's accent—an utterly objective and random event—that evoked in me an aggregate of troublesome racial emotions. The accent was a correlative to those emotions by virtue of association alone." (1990:153)

I strongly suspect that many people may have similar reactions upon hearing nonstandard English, be it vernacular African American English or some other nonstandard dialect belonging to some other linguistically disenfranchised group. Steele's reaction to a white southern accent may be akin to some negative Ebonics reactions. Considering the nature of race relations in this country, particularly as they have evolved since emancipation, is it possible that a black "accent" might evoke "emotions by virtue of association alone"? Vociferous public reactions to Ebonics would suggest that the answer is yes, and therein lie the larger issues regarding efforts to enhance national unity that are the ultimate motivation for this discussion.

For far too long the quest for racial equity has pushed hot buttons like affirmative action, while ignoring the importance of corresponding linguistic buttons altogether; that cycle must be broken if race relations in this country are ever to improve. Toward this end I would like to share a personal anecdote that differs considerably from Steele's racially charged reaction to southern speech. It is deeply personal and grows from my first extensive encounter with a special brand of southern speech, which I first encountered upon moving to Texas in 1979.

I grew up in Philadelphia and Los Angeles. My first linguistic exposure was in a socially stratified African American community in which my parents, as college graduates, were among the most highly educated people in our neighborhood (see chapter 1). Like Richard Rodriguez (1981), I began to observe differences in public versus private linguistic behavior. But unlike Rodriguez's experience in a Spanish-speaking family, my parents would engage in dialect style shifting on various occasions, and I eventually began to associate standard English with conversations that took place among whites who lived outside our black neighborhood. Nonstandard African American vernacular English was spoken—often with considerable pride—in the womb of our local African American community. Many neighbors with whom we attended church made still further linguistic distinctions between the street dialect, or black street speech (Baugh 1983), and the home language, which was devoid of "foul language" or other "bad words."

Beyond the use or nonuse of taboo words lay more subtle linguistic distinctions, and one of the earliest linguistic features I consciously controlled in the presence of blacks or whites was my use—or lack of use— of "y'all." I learned, thanks to the diligent efforts of my parents, that "you" (singular or plural) was proper and should be used in school and on formal occasions. They made no direct comments about "y'all," but I soon concluded that if I planned to use "y'all" I had better do so outside school or during informal discussions when my language would not be harshly judged. When we moved to California in 1958, I observed similar lines of linguistic demarcation pertaining to "y'all" among blacks and "you" among whites, but I no longer observed working-class whites using "yous," as I had in Philadelphia (for example, "Are yous going to the store?" versus "Are y'all going to the store?" versus "Are you going to the store?").

When I returned from California to Philadelphia in 1970, to attend college and graduate school, these lines of linguistic sedimentation were etched in my mind, as was my tendency to accommodate my use of "y'all" or "you" to conform with the racial configuration of the group to which I was speaking. Upon completion of my doctorate at the University of Pennsylvania, I had the extreme good fortune of receiving several excellent job offers, including one from the University of Texas, which I eagerly accepted. During one of my first meetings with univer-

sity officials and alumni, traveling by riverboat along the banks of beau-
tiful Lake Austin, I was stunned—and pleased—when a distinguished
alumnus took an interest in my housing predicament, "Well, . . . do y'all
think y'all want to buy a house right away?"

Despite my effort at restraint, I couldn't help but react to his use
of "y'all"; never having previously spent extensive time in the South, I
simply hadn't encountered "y'all" usage among whites before moving to
Texas. In contrast to Shelby Steele's sense of racist foreboding, I felt a
sense of linguistic liberation once I encountered "y'all" usage among
well-educated white Texans, along with some other nonstandard forms
I had used exclusively with fellow African Americans, such as "fixin' to,"
as in "We're fixin' to go to the store."

Far from reviving memories of the old South, with its entrenched
racial prejudice, I felt a welcoming sense of linguistic kinship among
fellow Texans, most of whom were keenly aware—as Lyndon Johnson
privately attested—that people in other parts of the United States often
mocked Texans' speech. I never shared negative stereotypes toward "los
lenguas Tejanos" (the Texas languages), and I welcomed the relaxed
linguistic atmosphere that I quickly began to associate with the can-do
spirit that at the time was lubricated by a massive Texas oil boom. My
positive linguistic experience in Texas, reinforced by my knowledge of
the South, helped me avoid the misguided linguistic stereotypes that
consumed Shelby Steele. His admission of linguistic prejudice alerts us
to such bias within the Ebonics debate, where linguistic prejudice has
an inescapable racial dimension.

Steele's (1990) confession of linguistic prejudice, or, more precisely,
his inclination toward a racist reaction to white Southern speech, belies
his comments on Ebonics, where he states, "In the interest of self-
esteem, of protecting black children from racial shame, Ebonics makes
broken English the equivalent of standard English" (Steele 1997:B7). In
table 1 (see chapter 8), standard English is contrasted with nonstandard
English, but not with "broken English." "Broken English" contrasts with,
what? "fixed English"? Also, African American educational success need
not come at the cost of misguided racial or linguistic shame, and here
Steele's (1990) autobiographical confessions are indicative of a deeper
personal linguistic trauma that we can hope will never afflict future
generations of black students, or students from any other linguistic back-

ground. Upon learning that a white woman had been critical of his teenage speech, Steele confides that he "felt racial shame at this white woman's fastidious concern with my language" (Steele 1990:58).

Although there is absolutely no reason to doubt that Steele, betrayed by latent traces of his youthful African American dialect, truly felt racial shame, educators would be ill advised to invoke linguistic shame in the name of black academic advancement. Steele's adolescent speech probably called even greater attention to itself because he belonged to a racially integrated swim team. Be that as it may, there is absolutely no reason to conclude that his shame-induced embrace of standard English is deserving of educational replication. For no child should be made to feel the weight of racial shame that Steele found to be so painful:

> Rather than feel racial shame, I recomposed this situation into a tableau of racial victimization in which this woman openly scorned my race. (1990:58) . . .

> she had grown up poor, had never finished high school, and would never be more than a secretary. She said she didn't give a "good goddamn" about my race, but that if I wanted to do more than "sweat my life away in a steel mill," I better learn to speak correctly." (1990:60)

I too have known the pain of insensitive remarks about black speech, and I believe that Steele's racial shame was tied closely to a coexistent sense of linguistic vulnerability. This issue may be even more pronounced for biracial children of black and white parentage, perhaps due to bicultural linguistic exposure. Steele is certainly not alone regarding his abiding sense of linguistic shame. Sowell described similar experiences, albeit entirely within an African American context: "Although we were all black kids in Harlem, I was from the South and talked 'funny' and everybody 'knew' that Southern kids were 'dumb'—and reminded me at every opportunity" (1972:5).

Despite this personal experience, Sowell (1997) took some satirical swipes at Ebonics: "If you think 'Ebonics' or 'black English' is an ill-conceived attempt to educate black children, you are very mistaken. It is a well-conceived way for the Oakland school board to evade responsibility for bad academic results and to get federal money" (1997:15A).

He continues with comparisons with other immigrants, and in so doing he inadvertently lends renewed credence to calls for racial resegregation in schools:

> The "ulterior motives" gambit came right after Cook of the Oakland School Board, was asked a very straightforward question by a reporter who said it was the traditional immigrant experience for children to come from homes where people did not speak standard English, but that such children did not cling to the language patterns of their elders.
>
> Nothing will get the excuse-mongers' backs up faster than comparing black children with immigrant children, but if such comparisons are racist, just call me a racist. I did a study making such a comparison more than 20 years ago, using records from the 1940s on the test scores in Harlem schools and in schools on the lower east side of New York where the children of immigrants went. Whether it was word meaning, paragraph meaning or mathematics, the children in the Harlem schools generally did just as well as the children in the schools on the lower east side. Sometimes the Harlem children did a little better, sometimes the lower east side children did a little better, but it was neck and neck. In those days, excuses about "black English" were unnecessary because black students were not miles behind everybody else, as they are too often today.

First, I absolutely agree with the last point; most black students are still too far behind. Closing educational gaps is a good starting point, but nothing less than the elimination of the racial chasm in academic performance will completely abolish the need for affirmative action or other remedies to overcome the history of unequal educational opportunities. I therefore believe linguistic (re?)unification among Americans must begin by reaffirming that the linguistic experience of the children of "traditional immigrants" and that of children who are American slave descendants is fundamentally different, as indicated in my response to Brent Staples's (1997) unfortunate remarks about "street English" and "broken inner-city English" (see preface):

> Whereas typical European immigrants may have come to the United States in poverty, speaking a language other than English, they were not enslaved captives who were isolated from other speakers of their

native language, which was a practice employed by slave traders to prevent revolts. Nor were they denied statutory access to schools, literacy or judicial relief in the courts. (Baugh 1997, p. A20)

As for the better academic performance of African American students during the Harlem Renaissance in the 1940s, those educational accomplishments were produced in racially segregated schools. At the 1997 national gathering of the National Association for the Advancement of Colored People (NAACP), challenges to the monolithic efforts toward full racial integration were challenged. Some argued that Afrocentric schools for African American children might produce better educational results than have most schools since *Brown v. Board of Education,* that is, long after the segregated educational era that Sowell describes.

The topic of the potential benefits of educational resegregation for black students was played out during an episode of a January 23, 1997, Gordon Elliot television show on Ebonics, on which I was one of several guests. Another guest, Professor Richard Wright of Howard University, was most outspoken in recalling his own childhood education in racially segregated schools in Texas:

> PROFESSOR WRIGHT: I wanted to make a statement that the whole problem of black children going to school and not learning standard English is a relatively recent phenomenon. It is not the case that black people used to go to school came out the way they went in, okay? I went to school during the 1940s and 50s. We didn't go to school as speakers of black English. We went to school understanding that the purpose of school was to clean up whatever you took in. . . . Since desegregation you've had to deal with the weight of color. When we went to school, we just went to school. You didn't go to school as a black child, you just went to school as a child.
> GORDON: Is this whole thing "race"? I mean, I don't see anybody talking about "good old boys" getting through school.
> PROFESSOR WRIGHT: I'd like to say that the weight of race is something black people have to carry today. When I went to school I did not carry the weight of race.
> GORDON: Because . . . ?
> PROFESSOR WRIGHT: Because I went to a school, I did not go to a black school, I just went to school.

GORDON: You were in an all-black classroom? You all had to get through what you had to get through. No racial issue was involved?

PROFESSOR WRIGHT: During the period of segregation.. During the period of segregation there was not such a thing in your mind as you were going to a black school.

GORDON: Right.

PROFESSOR WRIGHT: You were simply going to school and the assumption was that you were going to school because you had something to do there you couldn't do away from school, and that's learn something.

GORDON: I hear you, but you can't roll back the clock. I mean, we are where we are now.

PROFESSOR WRIGHT: No, but what we need to understand is that there is an environment in school in which race is something you have to deal with while you're trying to learn something.

When Sowell rolled back the clock, looking for evidence of superior black academic performance, ironically he found it within Harlem's racially segregated schools at the tail end of the war economy of the 1940s. I say "ironically" because it is readily apparent that evidence of this kind could easily lend considerable credence to calls for racially resegregated education. Sowell's evidence confirms that black students who were once isolated from white students thrived in relative comparison to their contemporary peers who have suffered greater academic declines. I suspect that Sowell had not considered the prospect of his studies' lending support to calls for resegregated American schools, but until such time as we not just close but eliminate gaps in educational performance between wealthy and economically poor students, then calls for resegregated schools are likely to continue—and grow louder.

I believe that America's higher education system offers a good educational model for African Americans. Black students who are interested in higher education have a choice between historically black colleges or universities or institutions of higher learning where blacks remain in the minority. These are authentic educational choices, and both educational options increase advanced African American educational opportunities. If a similar philosophy were extended to K–12 education, then another educational picture emerges; it is not one that neither favors nor condemns racially segregated or desegregated schools in an a priori manner. What is far more important is that schools be successful whatever the racial or linguistic composition of their student body.

Whereas the notions of academic excellence, racial harmony, and greater acceptance of linguistic diversity are tightly intertwined, in the absence of a common crisis we Americans are rarely as closely interconnected as our cherished national creed implies—the creed that beckons to countless waves of immigrants still "yearning to breathe free." But direct linguistic comparisons with other immigrants, however appealing, can easily lead to some of the same false linguistic conclusions that Sowell surmised by "comparing black children with immigrant children." Steele repeats this same mistake when he suggests "that Asians came to this country with values well suited to the challenges and opportunities of freedom" (1990:69).

Readers who know something of various "Asian" cultures will recognize that maintenance of their native language and the preservation of racial purity were high among the cultural traits brought to the United States from China, Japan, Korea, and other Asian nations. Ogbu (1992) has nevertheless observed that Korean students in Japan do far less well academically than do their counterparts in the United States—why? Does it have something to do with "values well suited to the challenges and opportunities of freedom"—or with the fact that Koreans are victims of more hostile discrimination in Japan? Asian immigrants, like their European counterparts, came to this country with their language and culture reasonably intact, whether they were wealthy immigrants from Hong Kong or destitute refugees from Vietnam or Cambodia. One need only have scant knowledge of U.S. linguistic history to know that it was only the African slaves who were abruptly cut off from their linguistic heritage. This accounts for the fact that it was only African slaves, and their descendants, who were unable to establish transitional ethnolinguistic communities through efforts to preserve their indigenous languages. As human chattel, slaves were unlike any other immigrants because they had no direct control over their linguistic, educational, or personal destiny.

When immigrants from Sweden, Italy, Poland, Germany, Hungary, or Ireland first came to America they brought their native languages and customs with them. Often they were poor, or even destitute, arriving in New York without proper documentation, and they were often victimized by unscrupulous bigots beyond the sanctuary of "the old neighborhood," or by ruthless thugs from within their midst. Readers who live in one of the original thirteen former colonies will recognize vestiges of such ethnic enclaves that still exist in many of the older neighborhoods. It typically took, and takes, about three generations for an immigrant family to melt into the American pot, at least from a linguistic point of view. Why, then, as Steele and Sowell independently suggest, has it taken so much longer for slave descendants to complete this transition?

Racism is almost too easy to blame, and the outstanding work of leading sociologists (Bobo 1983; Sears 1973; Wilson 1996) suggest that overt racism is declining in favor of forms of symbolic and economic racism that still have the same intended exclusionary effects. How then do we challenge misconceptions about "Ebonics or the kinds of belligerence, paranoid, and provincial attitudes being promoted by race hustlers" (Sowell 1997, p. 5A) of every political persuasion? Enhanced linguistic awareness and a better understanding of the linguistic consequences of American slavery represent important new beginnings for racial healing. Part of that healing began when Oakland decided not to pursue its Ebonics agenda. Without fanfare or the potential embarrassment of a public apology, Oakland educators quietly dropped all references to Ebonics in their reformulated educational plans. Several linguists, myself included, were subsequently called on by the national media for reactions to the demise of Ebonics in Oakland. In an article in the May 6, 1997, *New York Times*, "Ebonics Omitted in Oakland Report of Teaching English," I concluded that Oakland educators "realized they were in a political box, and they had to do something to get out of it. I'm sure they're trying to implement a plan without igniting any further controversy" (Applebome 1997b, p. A19).

Other scholars were less circumspect, some going so far as to suggest that the entire Ebonics episode had more to do with Louis Farrakhan than it did with the educational welfare of black children. In actuality, this was not the case. Minister Farrakhan found himself in an unenviable political tug-of-war between both the two sides of the Ebonics debate. He clearly places value on the use of standard American English because, like Malcolm X before him, he devoted considerable attention to mastering it, and much of his power to lead grows directly from his considerable proficiency in it. Yet some of the most outspoken supporters of Ebonics are active members of the Nation of Islam.

Far from having inordinate influence over Oakland's Ebonics assertions, Farrakhan did everything he could to sidestep the Ebonics controversy, because any stand he took would have placed him in a no-win situation. Had he denounced standard English he would have appeared to be a linguistic hypocrite, but if he denounced Ebonics he could have easily angered many of his followers within the Nation of Islam, many of whom found the Afrocentric foundation of Ebonics to be in keeping with their own Pan African philosophy. Unlike Jesse Jackson, who dove into the Ebonics frenzy at the first available opportunity, only to flip-flop after closed door meetings with Oakland educational officials, Farrakhan was less conspicuous because the Ebonics tinderbox was even more volatile within the black community than might otherwise have been evident to those who lack frequent exposure to African Americans or our broad range of opinions on various topics (Gates 1994).

One of the main reasons conservative African American pundits have reacted so negatively to Ebonics grows from their nearly uniform sense of linguistic shame about their heritage. Steele's explicit admission of racial shame, previously described, merely reinforces this derogatory linguistic mythology. In contrast to the uninformed linguistic opinions of self-reflecting African American pundits lies a more ominous legal forecast, because the mere evaporation of Ebonics from Oakland's educational agenda does not remove the underlying linguistic dilemma articulated in the first place. Far too many African American students continue to lag behind their white and Asian counterparts, and just because Ebonics is no longer grabbing front-page headlines does not mean that the linguistic and educational needs of African American students are no longer worthy of educational or legal consideration. In fact, because these matters were dropped rather than resolved, it is probably only a matter of time before we once again ponder the legal and educational consequences of American slavery.

Some of these very same linguistic concerns surfaced during the early phases of Clarence Thomas's U.S. Senate confirmation hearings. Were I to advise future attorneys who might yet have the opportunity to argue the legal and educational merits of African American English before the Supreme Court, I would strongly encourage them to consult

transcripts of Thomas's confirmation hearings, paying particular attention to questions posed by former Senator Howard Heflin.

At that time, Senator Heflin was the senior senator from Alabama,
and he spoke with the very kind of heavy southern accent to which
Steele (1990) alluded. During some genial testimony Senator Heflin
asked Justice Thomas, then citizen Thomas, about his undergraduate
education. The atmosphere was cordial and lighthearted as Justice Thomas replied that he had "majored in English." He then went on to
explain that he had done so on the advice of elementary school teachers
who had informed him that he spoke "a foreign language." Most people
gathered at the hearing shared a laugh and seemed mildly amused by
his revelation. None challenged his assertion, nor did they scoff at the
suggestion that a teacher might tell a black student that she or he spoke
"a foreign language." In the wake of the Ebonics controversy, however,
Justice Thomas's motivation to become an English major, thereby allow-
ing him to "learn English as a second language," reveals the depths of
misunderstanding about the linguistic legacy of American slavery. Such
attitudes and impressions are only a backdrop to a much larger land-
scape.

Should black English ever become a topic of consideration for the
U.S. Supreme Court, it will be interesting to see how Justice Thomas
reacts to the issue. Will he recall his childhood, and the anguish derived
from a foreboding sense of linguistic inadequacy? Or will he conclude,
as Sowell has, that African Americans are fundamentally no different
from any other group of immigrants but for the stereotype that the vast
majority of blacks have yet to demonstrate the necessary will, desire,
and tenacity to compete, without affirmative action crutches, in a free
market economy. The future holds the answer to this hypothetical scenario, but those who recognize the unique linguistic history of American
slaves and their descendants can do much to help this nation toward
racial reconciliation.

As a linguist I have found the entire Ebonics episode fascinating.
Feeling somewhat like a linguistic gumshoe, it has been a stimulating
intellectual exercise to trace the evolution of Ebonics from its birth in
St. Louis in 1973 through its global Oakland debut to its ultimate educational repudiation. However, I do not live in a linguistic vacuum,
and my concern for the well-being of all people begins at home.

In my role as a father of children who still face an uncertain racial future, I shall continue to work tirelessly toward the rapid demise of racism, and the elimination of misplaced linguistic chauvinism is part of this enterprise. In my role as an African American I share many of the frustrations that other American slave descendants feel upon witnessing multifarious forms of racial injustice. As an African American linguist who studies the evolution of linguistic diversity and its relevance to policy issues in education and the law, I remain keenly aware of the need to inform others of the fact that all human languages and dialects are equal in the eyes of science, even if they are not considered to be equal in the eyes of the law.

In my cherished civic role, however, as an American citizen, I ultimately seek the betterment of the entire nation where success for some need not come at the cost of failure for others, where greed and avarice need not outweigh generosity and compassion. Political leaders and aspirants who advocate strong commitments to educational advancement and improved race relations will find that these disparate social strands are intertwined within the Ebonics debate, and the available evidence clearly suggests that racism tenaciously persists as one of the most insidious carcinogenic tumors that still infect ailing portions of the body politic. I therefore eagerly seek the day when we all finally dismantle the unspoken "gentlemen's agreements" that have heretofore served to divide us. History demonstrates that we are at our weakest when we allow bigotry to reinforce superficial differences that stand as barriers to our collective well-being.

A new tolerance will demand that people from different backgrounds find ways to work together as cohesive and effective teams, capable of setting aside cultural, political, and linguistic differences in subordination to a higher common good. When compared with so many of the other important issues that occupy our daily lives, I know that Ebonics, and other possible sources of linguistic strife, make up only a small portion of the larger social, political, and economic puzzle, where hunger, health, and habitat are far more pressing to the vast majority of poor Americans than whether or not they say "aks" versus "ask."

In addition to important efforts to help students master standard English (efforts that should be modified as necessary to serve students from diverse linguistic backgrounds), new efforts are necessary to broaden existing curricula to teach more Americans about their fascinating linguistic heritage. Indeed, an honest portrayal of the rich linguistic history of the United States has the potential to introduce American linguistic diversity to students in an enticing multicultural format that includes every person in the United States. The envisioned multicultural curriculum need not take on the dreaded form of politically correct dogmatic enlightenment but, rather, can be tailored to each school—and those schools can in turn be linked to their local school districts, which in turn can be connected to their respective states, which in turn can share their linguistic legacy with pride to the entire nation. Such a venture might eventually allow us to invert the exclusionary linguistic traditions of the past with new efforts to help students preserve languages other than English (which are vital to our national welfare in the current global economy), as they come to learn standard American English to the best of their ability as rapidly as possible. Through positive, linguistically unifying efforts we may finally stir from the decades-long slumber of Dr. King's dream to the dawn of a new awakening. Only then will this nation of racially diverse citizens eventually achieve her color-blind ambition.

Linguistic Society of America Resolution on the Oakland "Ebonics" Issue

LSA Resolution on the Oakland "Ebonics" Issue

Whereas there has been a great deal of discussion in the media and among the American public about the 18 December 1996 decision of the Oakland School Board to recognize the language variety spoken by many African American students and to take it into account in teaching Standard English, the Linguistic Society of America, as a society of scholars engaged in the scientific study of language, hereby resolves to make it known that:

a. The variety known as "Ebonics," "African American Vernacular English" (AAVE), and "Vernacular Black English" and by other names is systematic and rule-governed like all natural speech varieties. In fact all human linguistic systems— spoken, signed, and written—are fundamentally regular. The systematic and expressive nature of the grammar and pronunciation patterns of the African American vernacular has been established by numerous scientific studies over the past thirty years. Characterizations of Ebonics as "slang," "mutant," "lazy," "defective," "ungrammatical," or "broken English" are incorrect and demeaning.

b. The distinction between "languages" and "dialects" is usually made more on social and political grounds than on purely linguistic ones. For example, different varieties of Chinese are popularly regarded as "dialects," though their speakers cannot understand each other, but speakers of Swedish and Norwegian, which are regarded as separate "languages," generally understand each other. What is important from a linguistic and educational point of view is not whether AAVE is called a "language" or a "dialect" but rather that its systematicity be recognized.

c. As affirmed in the LSA Statement of Language Rights (June 1996), there are individual and group benefits to maintaining vernacular speech varieties and there are scientific and human advantages to linguistic diversity. For those living in the United States there are also benefits in acquiring Standard English and resources should be made available to all who aspire to mastery of Standard English. The Oakland School Board's commitment to helping students master Standard English is commendable.

d. There is evidence from Sweden, the US. and other countries that speakers of other varieties can be aided in their learning of the standard variety by pedagogical approaches which recognize the legitimacy of the other varieties of a language. From this perspective, the Oakland School Board's decision to recognize the vernacular of African American students in teaching them Standard English is linguistically and pedagogically sound.

Chicago, Illinois
January 1997

A P P E N D I X   B

Texas 75th Legislature, Regular Session: House Resolution 28

THE STATE OF TEXAS
BILL TEXT
STATENET
Copyright (©) 1997 by Information for Public Affairs, Inc.
TEXAS 75TH LEGISLATURE—REGULAR SESSION
HOUSE RESOLUTION 28
1997 TX H.R. 28

VERSION: Introduced
VERSION-DATE: January 16, 1997
SYNOPSIS:

Resolution

TEXT: Whereas, Mastery of the English language is absolutely vital to students in the public school system and;

1997 TX H.R. 28

Whereas, Each and every child in Texas should be given the opportunity and support necessary to become proficient with English as their primary language, and;

Whereas, Many students in Texas do not utilize standard English to communicate, some of these students are African-Americans and use a derivative of Pan African dialects sometimes referred to as Ebonics as a means of communication, and;

Whereas, It is often difficult for teachers to understand this dialect and therefore difficult to teach these students in an academic setting, and;

Whereas, In order to be more effective and more successful with teaching these students both mastery of standard English and other subjects it is necessary to identify those students who utilized a Pan African dialect derivative as a method of communication, and;

Whereas, Focus on assisting teachers charged with educating these students must be an integral part of teaching them standard English. Teachers must be given the tools necessary to assist them in communication with these students, therefore be it;

1997 TX H.R. 28

Resolved that the Texas Education Agency is hereby requested to communicate with local school districts in the state regarding their identification of students that utilize Pan African dialect as a means of communication. Each district should be asked to report back to TEA the number of students in their district that utilize this dialect and, therefore be it further;

Resolved, that the Texas Education Agency work with local school districts so affected to develop a plan to assist teachers in these districts with communicating with students utilizing Pan African dialect derivative as a method of communication. It is the intent of the Legislature that this be accomplishedby using existing resources.

SPONSOR:
Wilson

A P P E N D I X   C

California 1997–98 Regular Session: Senate Bill 205

CALIFORNIA 1997–98 REGULAR SESSION
SENATE BILL 205
AMENDED IN SENATE MARCH 3, 1997

SENATE BILL   NO. 205

INTRODUCED BY SENATOR HAYNES
[A⟩ (PRINCIPAL COAUTHOR: SENATOR MOUNT JOY) ⟨A]
[A⟩ (COAUTHOR: SENATOR LEWIS) ⟨A]
[A⟩ (COAUTHORS: ASSEMBLY MEMBERS ASHBURN,
BALDWIN, BATTIN, FRUSETTA, GRANLUND, HOUSE,
KALOOGIAN, LEACH, LEONARD, MARGETT, MCCLINTOCK,
AND RUNNER) ⟨A]
JANUARY 28, 1997

1997 CA S.B. 205

VERSION: Amended

VERSION-DATE: March 3, 1997

SYNOPSIS:

An act to add Sections 31 and 32 to the Education Code, relating to education.

DIGEST:

LEGISLATIVE COUNSEL'S DIGEST

SB 205, as amended, Haynes. Education: Equality in English Instruction Act.

Existing law requires that English be the basic language of instruction in all public schools.

1997 CA S.B. 205

This bill would enact the "Equality in English Instruction Act." [A⟩ THE BILL WOULD REQUIRE THE STATE DEPARTMENT OF EDUCATION TO IMMEDIATELY TERMINATE THE PROFICIENCY IN STANDARD ENGLISH FOR SPEAKERS OF BLACK LANGUAGE PROGRAM, AS SPECIFIED. ⟨A] The bill would prohibit the state, its subdivisions, and local government agencies, including school districts and community college districts, from expending state funds or resources, or applying for federal funding, for the purpose of, or support for, [A⟩ THE PROVISION OF BLACK LANGUAGE, BLACK ENGLISH, OR ⟨A] Ebonics instruction, as defined. The bill would require that any funding that already has been obtained for the purpose of, or support for, [A⟩ THE PROVISION OF BLACK LANGUAGE, BLACK ENGLISH, OR ⟨A] Ebonics instruction be instead used for the classroom teaching of linguistic or communication skills in the English language. [D⟩ The ⟨D]

[A⟩ THIS ⟨A] bill would require the State Department of Education to submit written recommendations, within 90 days of the operative date of the bill, to the Legislature regarding the structure and implementation of a program that would provide financial incentives to school districts that [A⟩, USING ENGLISH LANGUAGE INSTRUCTION, ⟨A] improve linguistic or communication skills of students in low-income areas of the state and financial penalties for school districts where the skills have deteriorated, as measured by objective testing data, as specified.

Vote: majority. Appropriation: no. Fiscal committee: yes. State-mandated local program: no.

NOTICE:
[A⟩ UPPERCASE TEXT WITHIN THESE SYMBOLS IS ADDED ⟨A]
[D⟩ Text within these symbols is deleted ⟨D]

TEXT: THE PEOPLE OF THE STATE OF CALIFORNIA DO ENACT AS FOLLOWS:

[D⟩ SECTION 1. This act shall be known, and may be ⟨D]

[A⟩ SECTION 1. THIS ACT SHALL BE KNOWN, AND MAY BE CITED, AS THE "EQUALITY IN ENGLISH INSTRUCTION ACT."⟨A]

[A⟩ SEC. 2. SECTION 31 IS ADDED TO THE EDUCATION CODE, TO READ: ⟨A]

[A⟩ 31. (A) THE LEGISLATURE FINDS AND DECLARES ALL OF THE FOLLOWING: ⟨A]

[A⟩ (1) THE STATE DEPARTMENT OF EDUCATION'S PROFICIENCY IN STANDARD ENGLISH FOR SPEAKERS OF BLACK LANGUAGE PROGRAM DISTRIBUTES STAFF DEVELOPMENT AND LESSON PLAN MATERIALS TO SCHOOL DISTRICTS THAT EXPLICITLY DIRECT TEACHERS TO DO BOTH OF THE FOLLOWING: ⟨A]

[A⟩ (A) INCORPORATE SLANG INTO THEIR LESSON PLANS. ⟨A]

[A⟩ (B) TEACH THAT SLANG IS AN APPROPRIATE ALTER-NATIVE TO CORRECT ENGLISH IN SOME SITUATIONS. ⟨A]

[A⟩ (2) THE STATE DEPARTMENT OF EDUCATION'S PRO-FICIENCY IN STANDARD ENGLISH FOR SPEAKERS OF BLACK LANGUAGE PROGRAM RECOMMENDS THAT TEACHERS DO ALL OF THE FOLLOWING: ⟨A]

[A⟩ (A) ADVISE STUDENTS THAT USING SLANG IS MORE APPROPRIATE THAN USING CORRECT ENGLISH IN CERTAIN SITUATIONS. ⟨A]

[A⟩ (B) "KILL THE MYTH" THAT "STANDARD ENGLISH IS THE CORRECT WAY TO SPEAK AT ALL TIMES." ⟨A]

[A⟩ (C) "KILL THE MYTH" THAT "IN ORDER TO TEACH STANDARD ENGLISH, THE TEACHER MUST ERADICATE THE STUDENTS HOME LANGUAGE." ⟨A]

[A⟩ (D) SPEAK SPECIFIC SENTENCES TO THEIR STU-DENTS IN SLANG. ⟨A]

[A⟩ (E) MAKE AUDIO TAPES OF THEMSELVES SPEAKING IN SLANG. ⟨A]

[A⟩ (F) WRITE SENTENCES IN SLANG ON CHALKBOARDS AND OVERHEAD TRANSPARENCIES. ⟨A]

[A⟩ (3) GRANTING SLANG AN OFFICIAL PLACE IN CALI-FORNIA'S CLASSROOMS, AND DIRECTING TEACHERS TO IN-STRUCT STUDENTS THAT SLANG IS APPROPRIATE IN CER-TAIN
SITUATIONS, LEGITIMIZES INCORRECT ENGLISH. LEGITI-MIZING INCORRECT ENGLISH AS POLITICAL CORRECTNESS IS A DISSERVICE TO CHILDREN. ⟨A]

[A⟩ (4) AT LEAST ONE SCHOOL DISTRICT HAS ENACTED, AND OTHERS ARE CONTEMPLATING ENACTING, POLICIES

THAT EXPAND THE STATE DEPARTMENT OF EDUCATION'S PROFICIENCY IN STANDARD ENGLISH FOR SPEAKERS OF BLACK LANGUAGE PROGRAM IN ORDER TO TRAIN TEACHERS IN THE INSTRUCTIONAL STRATEGIES AND CURRICULUM RECOMMENDED BY THE STATE DEPARTMENT OF EDUCATION'S BLACK LANGUAGE PROGRAM. ⟨A]

[A⟩ (5) CALLING THEIR PROGRAMS "EBONICS," THESE DISTRICTS ARE ATTEMPTING TO CONVINCE STUDENTS THAT POOR COMMUNICATION SKILLS ARE ACCEPTABLE SPEECH PATTERNS AND WRITING SKILLS, AND THAT THESE STUDENTS CANNOT LEARN TO SPEAK CORRECT ENGLISH DUE TO SOCIAL OR CULTURAL FACTORS OUTSIDE THEIR CONTROL. THE JUSTIFICATION FOR "EBONICS" INSTRUCTION IS THE SAME AS THAT USED TO JUSTIFY SEPARATE EDUCATIONAL INSTITUTIONS FOR AFRICAN-AMERICANS PRIOR TO THE CASE OF BROWN V. BOARD OF EDUCATION. IT IS THE PERPETUATION OF THE "SEPARATE BUT EQUAL" PHILOSOPHY THAT HAS HARMED RACE RELATIONS IN THIS COUNTRY FOR FAR TOO MANY YEARS. ⟨A]

[A⟩ (B) IT IS THE INTENT OF THE LEGISLATURE, IN ENACTING THE ACT THAT ADDS THIS SECTION, THAT EVERY STUDENT, REGARDLESS OF RACE, COLOR, SEX, OR NATIONAL ORIGIN, BECOME PROFICIENT IN CORRECT ENGLISH AND OBTAIN THE LINGUISTIC AND COMMUNICATION SKILLS NECESSARY TO BECOME PRODUCTIVE MEMBERS OF CALIFORNIA'S COMMUNITIES. ⟨A]

[A⟩ (C) FOR THE PURPOSES OF THIS ARTICLE, "BLACK LANGUAGE INSTRUCTION," "BLACK ENGLISH INSTRUCTION," AND "EBONICS INSTRUCTION" SHALL INCLUDE ALL OF THE FOLLOWING: ⟨A]

[A⟩ (1) THE TEACHING IN SCHOOLS OF WHAT ITS ADHERENTS CALL AN AFRICAN-AMERICAN FOREIGN LANGUAGE, OR A DIALECT UNIQUE TO AFRICAN-AMERICANS, AS PART OF A BILINGUAL INSTRUCTION PROGRAM. ⟨A]

[A⟩ (2) THE TEACHING IN SCHOOLS OF WHAT ITS AD-HERENTS CALL AN AFRICAN-AMERICAN FOREIGN LAN-GUAGE, OR A DIALECT UNIQUE TO AFRICAN-AMERICANS, AS A LANGUAGE SEPARATE AND DISTINCT FROM ENGLISH. ⟨A]

[A⟩ (3) THE TRAINING OF TEACHERS OR ADMINISTRA-TIVE STAFF IN SCHOOLS TO SPEAK, WRITE, READ, OR UN-DERSTAND WHAT ITS ADHERENTS CALL AN AFRICAN-AMERICAN FOREIGN LANGUAGE, OR A DIALECT UNIQUE TO AFRICAN-AMERICANS. ⟨A]

[A⟩ (4) THE TRAINING OF TEACHERS OR ADMINISTRA-TIVE STAFF IN SCHOOLS TO INCORPORATE WHAT ITS AD-HERENTS CALL AN AFRICAN-AMERICAN FOREIGN LAN-GUAGE, OR A DIALECT UNIQUE TO AFRICAN-AMERICANS, INTO THEIR LESSON PLANS. ⟨A]

[A⟩ (5) THE TRAINING OF TEACHERS OR ADMINISTRA-TIVE STAFF IN SCHOOLS TO TEACH THAT WHAT ITS AD-HERENTS CALL AN AFRICAN-AMERICAN FOREIGN LAN-GUAGE, OR A DIALECT UNIQUE TO AFRICAN-AMERICANS, IS AN APPROPRIATE ALTERNATIVE TO CORRECT ENGLISH IN SOME SITUATIONS. ⟨A]

[A⟩ SEC. 3. SECTION 32 IS ADDED TO THE EDUCATION CODE, TO READ: ⟨A]

[A⟩ 32. NOTWITHSTANDING ANY OTHER PROVISION OF LAW: ⟨A]

[A⟩ (A) (1) THE STATE DEPARTMENT OF EDUCATION SHALL IMMEDIATELY TERMINATE THE PROFICIENCY IN STANDARD ENGLISH FOR SPEAKERS OF BLACK LANGUAGE

PROGRAM. NO STATE FUNDS OR RESOURCES, OR STATE-DERIVED FUNDS OR RESOURCES, SHALL BE USED FOR, OR IN SUPPORT OF, THE PROFICIENCY IN STANDARD ENGLISH FOR SPEAKERS OF BLACK LANGUAGE PROGRAM. ⟨A]

[A⟩ (2) NO STATE EMPLOYEE, INCLUDING ANY PERSON UNDER THE AUTHORITY OF THE STATE DEPARTMENT OF EDUCATION OR THE SUPERINTENDENT OF PUBLIC INSTRUCTION, SHALL OPERATE, SUPPORT, OR COORDINATE, OR CONTRIBUTE TO THE OPERATION, SUPPORT, OR COORDINATION OF THE PROFICIENCY IN STANDARD ENGLISH FOR SPEAKERS OF BLACK LANGUAGE PROGRAM, OR PROVIDE OR SUPPORT BLACK LANGUAGE INSTRUCTION OR BLACK ENGLISH INSTRUCTION OR EBONICS INSTRUCTION IN THE STATE OF CALIFORNIA, EVEN IF HIS OR HER SALARY IS PROVIDED, IN FULL OR IN PART, BY FEDERAL FUNDS. ⟨A]

[A⟩ (B) NEITHER THE STATE, NOR ANY OF ITS SUBDIVISIONS, NOR ANY LOCAL GOVERNMENT AGENCIES IN CALIFORNIA, INCLUDING THE STATE DEPARTMENT OF EDUCATION AND SCHOOL DISTRICTS, SHALL UTILIZE STATE FUNDS OR RESOURCES, OR STATE-DERIVED FUNDS OR RESOURCES, FOR THE PURPOSE OF, OR SUPPORT FOR, PROVIDING BLACK LANGUAGE INSTRUCTION, BLACK ENGLISH INSTRUCTION, OR EBONICS INSTRUCTION. ⟨A]

[A⟩ (C) NEITHER THE STATE, NOR ANY OF ITS SUBDIVISIONS, NOR ANY LOCAL GOVERNMENT AGENCIES IN CALIFORNIA, INCLUDING SCHOOL DISTRICTS AND COMMUNITY COLLEGE DISTRICTS, SHALL APPLY FOR FEDERAL FUNDING FOR THE PURPOSE OF, OR SUPPORT FOR, PROVIDING BLACK LANGUAGE INSTRUCTION, BLACK ENGLISH INSTRUCTION, OR EBONICS INSTRUCTION. ⟨A]

[A⟩ (D) UPON THE OPERATIVE DATE OF THE ACT THAT ADDS THIS SECTION, ANY STATE FUNDING THAT ALREADY

HAS BEEN OBTAINED FOR THE PURPOSE OF, OR SUPPORT FOR, PROVIDING BLACK LANGUAGE INSTRUCTION OR BLACK ENGLISH INSTRUCTION OR EBONICS INSTRUCTION, SHALL INSTEAD BE USED FOR THE CLASSROOM TEACHING OF LINGUISTIC OR COMMUNICATIONS SKILLS SOLELY IN THE ENGLISH LANGUAGE. ⟨A]

[A⟩ (E) WITHIN 90 DAYS AFTER THE OPERATIVE DATE OF THE ACT THAT ADDS THIS SECTION, THE STATE DEPART-MENT OF EDUCATION SHALL SUBMIT WRITTEN RECOM-MENDATIONS TO THE LEGISLATURE REGARDING THE STRUCTURE AND IMPLEMENTATION OF A PROGRAM THAT WOULD ACCOMPLISH EACH OF THE FOLLOWING: ⟨A]

[A⟩ (1) PROVIDE FINANCIAL INCENTIVES TO SCHOOL DISTRICTS THAT, USING ENGLISH LANGUAGE INSTRUC-TION, IMPROVE THE ENGLISH LANGUAGE SKILLS OF STU-DENTS IN LOW-INCOME AREAS OF THE STATE, AND FINAN-CIAL PENALTIES FOR SCHOOL DISTRICTS WHERE THESE SKILLS HAVE DETERIORATED, AS MEASURED BY OBJECTIVE TESTING DATA. ⟨A]

[A⟩ (2) BE FUNDED FROM READING AND PHONICS FUNDS APPROPRIATED FOR THE PURPOSE OF INCREASING READING, WRITING, OR COMMUNICATION SKILL LEVELS IN THE STATE OF CALIFORNIA. ⟨A] [D⟩ cited, as the "Equality in English Instruction Act." ⟨D]

[D⟩ SEC. 2. Section 31 is added to the Education Code, to read: ⟨D]

[D⟩ 31. (a) The Legislature finds and declares all of the following: ⟨D]

[D⟩ (1) Linguistic skills, including reading, writing, and speaking proper and effective English, are the key to an individual's success in work and in the community. The ability to effectively communicate with others is the single most important factor in career development and advancement. ⟨D]

[D⟩ (2) The primary responsibility of the education system, and the schools in that system, is to prepare students for career success and equal participation in their community. ⟨D]

[D⟩ (3) At least one school district has enacted, and others are contemplating enacting, a district policy that seeks to justify the teaching of poor linguistic skills and perpetuates, intentionally or inadvertently, stereotypes about speech patterns and language and communication skills among certain sectors of society under the guise of a bilingual program. Calling the program "Ebonics" instruction, these districts are attempting to convince students that poor communication skills are acceptable speech patterns and writing skills, and that these students cannot learn to speak correct English due to cultural factors outside their control. ⟨D]

[D⟩ (4) The justification for "Ebonics" instruction is the same as that used to justify prohibiting language instruction to slaves, and to justify separate educational institutions for African-Americans prior to the case of Brown v. Board of Education. It is the perpetuation of the "separate but equal" philosophy that has harmed race relations in this country for far too many years. ⟨D]

[D⟩ (b) It is, therefore, the intent of the Legislature, in enacting the act that adds this section, that every student, regardless of race, color, sex, or national origin, become proficient in English and obtain the linguistic and communication skills necessary to become productive members of California's communities. ⟨D]

[D⟩ (c) For the purposes of this article, "Ebonics," or "Ebonics instruction," shall refer to what its adherents call the teaching of an African-American foreign language, or a dialect unique to African-

Americans in schools, as a language separate and distinct from English, or as a part of a bilingual instruction program. ⟨D]

[D⟩ SEC. 3. Section 32 is added to the Education Code, to read: ⟨D]

[D⟩ 32. Notwithstanding any other provision of law: ⟨D]

[D⟩ (a) Neither the state, nor any of its subdivisions, nor any local government agencies in California, including school districts and community college districts, shall utilize state funds or resources, or state-derived funds or resources, for the purpose of so-called Ebonics instruction or support for Ebonics instruction. ⟨D]

[D⟩ (b) Neither the state, nor any of its subdivisions, nor any local government agencies in California, including school districts and community college districts, shall apply for federal funding for so-called Ebonics instruction or support for Ebonics instruction. ⟨D]

[D⟩ (c) Upon the operative date of the act that adds this section, any state funding that already has been obtained for so-called Ebonics instruction, or support for Ebonics instruction, shall instead be used for the classroom teaching of linguistic or communication skills in the English language. ⟨D]

[D⟩ (d) Within 90 days after the operative date of the act that adds this section, the State Department of Education shall submit written recommendations to the Legislature regarding the structure and implementation of a program that would accomplish both of the following: ⟨D]

[D⟩ (1) Provide financial incentives to school districts that improve linguistic or communication skills of students in low-income areas of the state, and financial penalties for school districts where these skills have deteriorated, as measured by objective testing data. ⟨D]

[D⟩ (2) Be funded from reading and phonics funds appropriated for the purposeof increasing reading, writing, or communication skill levels in the State of California. ⟨D]

SPONSOR:
Haynes

References

Applebome, Peter. (1997a, May 6). "'Ebonics' Omitted in Oakland Report on Teaching English." *New York Times*, p. A19.

———. (1996b, December 20). "School District Elevates Status of Black English." *New York Times*, p. A18.

Asante, Molefe. (1979, June). "Editor's Statement: Ebonics (Black English): Implications for Education." *Journal of Black Studies* 9 (no. 4): 363.

Baugh, John. (1983). *Black Street Speech: Its History, Structure, and Survival.* Austin: University of Texas Press.

———. (1988). "Language and Race: Some Implications for Linguistic Science." In F. Newmeyer (ed.), *Linguistics: The Cambridge Survey*, vol. 4, pp. 64–74. Cambridge: Cambridge University Press.

———. (1991). "Changing Terms of Self-Reference among American Slave Descendants." *American Speech* 66 (no. 2): 133–46.

———. (1996). "Dimensions of a Theory of Econolinguistics." In Gregory Guy, Crawford Feagin, Deborah Schiffrin, and John Baugh (eds.), *A Social Science of Language*, pp. 397–419. Philadelphia: John Benjamins.

———. (1997, January 29). "Letters: Ebonics Isn't 'Street English' but a Heritage." *New York Times*, p. A20.

———. (1998). "Linguistics, Education, and the Law: Educational Reform for

African-American Language Minority Students." In Salikoko Mufwene, John Rickford, Guy Bailey, and John Baugh (eds.), *African-American English: Structure, History, and Use,* pp. 282–301. London: Routledge.

———. (1999). *Out of the Mouths of Slaves: African American Language and Educational Malpractice.* Austin: University of Texas Press.

Bereiter, C., and Engleman, S. (1966). *Teaching Disadvantaged Children in the Pre-School.* Englewood Cliffs, NJ: Prentice-Hall.

Bernstein, B. (1961). "Social Class and Linguistic Development: A Theory of Social Learning." In A. H. Halsey, J. Floud, and D. A. Anderson (eds.), *Education, Economy and Society,* pp. 288–314. New York: Free Press.

———. (1970). *Class, Codes, and Control. Theoretical Studies Towards a Sociology of Language,* vol. 1. London: Routledge & Kegan Paul.

Blackshire-Belay, Carol Aisha. (1996). "The Location of Ebonics within the Framework of the Africological Paradigm." *Journal of Black Studies* 27 (no. 1): 5–23.

Bloomfield, Leonard. (1933). *Language.* New York: Holt.

Bobo, Lawrence. (1983). "Whites' Opposition to Bussing: Symbolic Racism or Realistic Group Conflict?" *Journal of Personality and Social Psychology* 45: 1196–1210.

Brown v. Board of Education, 347 U.S. 483 (1954).

Chomsky, Noam. (1965). *Aspects of a Theory of Syntax.* Cambridge: MIT Press.

Cosby, William. (1997, January 10). "Elements of Igno-Ebonics Style." *Wall Street Journal,* p. A-11.

Coulmas, Florian. (1992). *Language and Economy.* Oxford: Blackwell.

Devlin, Desmond. (1997, April). "Hooked on Ebonics." *Mad Magazine,* p. 30.

Dillard, J. L. (1972). *Black English.* New York: Random House.

Du Bois, W. E. B. (1928). "The Name 'Negro.'" *The Crisis.* 35: 96–97.

"The Ebonics Virus." (1997, January 4). *The Economist,* p. 26.

Fordham, Signithia, and Ogbu, John. (1986). "Black Students' School Success: Coping with the Burden of 'Acting White.'" *The Urban Review* 8 (no. 3): 176–206.

Gates, Henry L. (1994). *Colored People.* New York: Knopf.

Gibbs, Jewelle. (1996). *Race and Justice.* San Francisco: Jossey-Bass.

Heilbrunn, Jacob. (1997, January 20). "Speech Therapy." *The New Republic* 279 (no. 4): 17–19.

Hernstein, Richard, and Murray, Charles. (1994). *The Bell Curve: Intelligence and Class Structure in American Life.* New York: Free Press.

Higgenbotham, A. Leon. (1978). *In the Matter of Color.* New York: Oxford University Press.

———. (1998). *Shades of Freedom.* New York: Oxford University Press.

Hoover, Mary Rhodes. (1998). "Ebonics: Myths and Realities." In Theresa Perry and Lisa Delpit (eds.), *The Real Ebonics Debate,* pp. 71–78. Boston: Beacon Press.

Jensen, Arthur. (1969). "How Much Can We Boost IQ?" *Harvard Educational Review* 39 (no. 1): 1–123.

Labov, William. (1966). *The Social Stratification of English in New York City.* Washington, DC: Center for Applied Linguistics.

———. (1969). "The Logic of Nonstandard English." In James Alatis (ed.), *Georgetown Monograph Series on Languages and Linguistics* 22: 1–44. Washington, DC: Georgetown University Press.

———. (1972). *Language in the Inner-City: Studies in the Black English Vernacular.* Philadelphia: University of Pennsylvania Press.

———. (1977, January 23). "Testimony before the U.S. Senate: Senate Appropriation Committee's Subcommittee on Labor, Health and Human Services, and Education, chaired by Senator Arlen Specter."

———. 1994. *Principles of Linguistic Change: Internal Factors.* Oxford: Blackwell.

Lau v. Nichols, 414 U.S. 563 (1974).

Leland, John, and Joseph, Nadine. (1997, January 13). "Hooked on Ebonics." *Newsweek,* pp. 78–79.

Lippi-Green, Rosina. (1997). *English with an Accent: Language, Ideology, and Discrimination in the United States.* London: Routledge.

McClaurin v. Oklahoma, 339 U.S. 637 (1950).

Newell, Peter. (1908). *The Hole Book.* New York: Harper & Brothers

Nunberg, Geoff. (1997). "Double Standards." *Natural Language and Linguistic Theory* 15 (no. 3): 667–675.

Ogbu, John. (1978). *Minority Education and Caste.* New York: Academic Press.

———. (1992). "Understanding Multicultural Education." *Educational Researcher* 21 (November): 5–14, 24.

O'Neil Wayne. (1998). "If Ebonics Isn't a Language, Then Tell Me, What Is? In Theresa Perry and Lisa Delpit (eds.), *The Real Ebonics Debate: Power, Language, and the Education of African American Children,* pp. 38–48. Boston: Beacon Press.

Orr, Elinor W. (1987). *Twice as Less: Black English and the Performance of Black Students in Mathematics and Science.* New York: Norton.

Perry, Theresa, and Delpit, Lisa (eds.). (1998). *The Real Ebonics Debate: Power, Language, and the Education of African American Children.* Boston: Beacon Press.

Plessy v. Ferguson, 163 U.S. 537 (1896).

Rodriguez, Richard. (1981). *Hunger of Memory.* New York: Bantam.

Sears, David (1973). *The Politics of Violence.* Boston: Houghton Mifflin.

Seymour, Harry, and Seymour, Charlana. (1979a). "Ebonics and P.L. 94–142."

In Gloria Tolliver-Weddington (ed.), *Ebonics (Black English): Implications for Education. Journal of Black Studies* 9 (no. 4): 449–468 [special issue].

———. (1979b). "The Symbolism of Ebonics: I'd Rather Switch than Fight." In Gloria Tolliver-Weddington (ed.), *Ebonics (Black English): Implications for Education. Journal of Black Studies* 9 (no. 4): 397–410 [special issue].

Shockley, William. (1972). "Dysgenics, Geneticity, Raceology: Challenges to the Intellectual Responsibility of Educators." *Phi Delta Kappan* 53 (no. 5).

Simpkins, Gary, and Holt, Grace. (1977). *The Bridge Program: A Cross-Cultural Reading Program.* Boston: Houghton Mifflin.

Sleeper, Jim. (1997). *Liberal Racism.* New York: Viking.

Smith, Ernie. (1975). "Ebonics: A Case History." In R. Williams (ed.), *Ebonics: The True Language of Black Folks.* pp. 77–85. St. Louis: Robert Williams and Associates.

———. (1992). "African American Language Behavior: A World of Difference." In Philip H. Dreywer (ed.), *Reading the World: Multimedia and Multicultural Learning in Today's Classroom* (56th yearbook of the Claremont Reading Conference), pp. 38–53. Claremont, CA: Claremont Reading Conference.

———(1998). "What Is Black English, What Is Ebonics?" In Theresa Perry and Lisa Delpit (eds.), *The Real Ebonics Debate: Power, Language, and the Education of African American Children,* pp. 49–58. Boston: Beacon Press.

Smitherman, Geneva. (1978). *Talkin' and Testifyin': The Language of Black America.* Boston: Houghton Mifflin.

———. (1991). "What Is Africa to Me?: Language, Ideology, and African American." *American Speech* 66 (no. 2): 115–132.

Sowell, Thomas. (1972). *Black Education: Myths and Tragedies.* New York: McKay.

———. (1997, February 13). "'Ebonics' Ploy a Good Way to Get Money." *Dayton Daily News.*

Staples, Brent. (1997, January 24). "The Last Train from Oakland." *New York Times,* p. A-30.

Steele, Shelby. (1990). *The Content of Our Character.* New York: St. Martin's Press.

———. (1997, January 15). "Black Pupils Deserve More from Schools than Ebonics." *Sacramento Bee,* p. B7.

Sweatt v. Painter, 339 US 629 (1950).

Tolliver-Weddington, Gloria (ed.). (1979). *Ebonics (Black English): Implications for Education. Journal of Black Studies* 9 (no. 4) [special issue].

Washington, Julie, and Craig, Holly. (1994). "Dialectal Forms during Discourse of Urban, African-American Preschoolers Living in Poverty." *Journal of Speech and Hearing Research* 37 (no. 8): 6–823.

Weinreich, Uriel. (1953). *Languages in Contact.* The Hague: Mouton.

Williams, Robert (ed.). (1975). *Ebonics: The True Language of Black Folks.* St. Louis: Robert Williams and Associates.

———. (1997a, January 28). "Ebonics as a Bridge to Standard English." *St. Louis Post-Dispatch,* p. A14.

———. (1997b, January 23). Testimony before the U.S. Senate: Senate Appropriation Subcommittee on Labor, Health and Human Services, and Education, chaired by Senator Arlen Specter.

———, and Rivers, L. Wendell. (1975). "The Effects of Language on the Test Performance of Black Children." In R. Williams (ed.), *Ebonics: The True Language of Black Folks,* pp. 96–109. St. Louis: Robert Williams & Associates.

Wilson, William J. (1996). *When Work Disappears: The World of the New Urban Poor.* New York: Knopf.

Wolfram, Walt, and Fasold, Ralph. (1969). "A Black English Translation of John 3:1–21 with Grammatical Annotations." *The Bible Translator* 20 (no. 2): 48–54.

Wright, George C. (1990). *Racial Violence in Kentucky: 1865–1940.* Baton Rouge: Louisiana State University Press.

Index